Modern Critical Views

ROBERT BROWNING

Edited with an introduction by

Harold Bloom

Sterling Professor of the Humanities
Yale University

1985
CHELSEA HOUSE PUBLISHERS
New York

THE COVER:
The cover represents the crisis of the solitary quester, Childe Roland, as he confronts the enigma of the Dark Tower while surrounded by the shades of all the lost adventurers, his peers.—H.B.

PROJECT EDITORS: Emily Bestler, James Uebbing
EDITORIAL COORDINATOR: Karyn Gullen Browne
EDITORIAL STAFF: Linda Grossman, Julia Myer, Peter Childers
DESIGN: Susan Lusk

Cover illustration by Kye Carbone

Printed and bound in the United States of America

Library of Congress Cataloging in Publication Data

Robert Browning.
    (Modern critical views)
    Bibliography: p.
    Includes index.
    1. Browning, Robert, 1812–1889—Criticism and
interpretation—Addresses, essays, lectures.
I. Bloom, Harold.   II. Series.
PR4238.R58   1985   821'.8   85–3799
ISBN 0–87754–614–2

Chelsea House Publishers
Harold Steinberg, Chairman and Publisher
Susan Lusk, Vice President
A Division of Chelsea House Educational Communications, Inc.
133 Christopher Street, New York, NY 10014

Modern Critical Views

ROBERT BROWNING

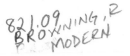
Contents

Editor's Note

This volume gathers together a representative selection of the best criticism devoted to Browning during the last quarter-century, arranged in the chronological order of their publication. It begins with the editor's "Introduction" emphasizing the uncanny problems clustering around Browning's concern for the self. Robert Langbaum's classical essay on the dramatic monologue begins the chronological sequence, and is followed by Isobel Armstrong's remarkable reading of "Mr. Sludge, 'The Medium',", with its hints of Browning's wager with nihilism. George Ridenour and John Hollander in different but related ways explore Browning's employment of music as both mode and trope. The essays on "Love Among the Ruins" and "A Toccata of Galuppi's" by Eleanor Cook, and on "Childe Roland" by the editor, open out upon the darknesses of Browning's relations to the dead and to literary history.

The remaining essays apply some modes of current advanced literary criticism to Browning. Ann Wordsworth's Lacanian analysis deconstructs Langbaum's empirical account of the dramatic monologue. The reading of "Cleon" by Herbert Tucker subtly relates Browning's poetics to his sense of the future, and to an art of the future. Finally, Steven Shaviro's account of "Caliban upon Setebos" strikingly compares Browning's critique of nihilism to both Nietzsche and Freud in their genealogies of guilt and of anxiety.

CHELSEA HOUSE PUBLISHERS
Modern Critical Views

Further titles in preparation.

Introduction

One of the principles of interpretation that will arise out of the future study of the intricacies of poetic revisionism, and of the kinds of misreading that canon-formation engenders, is the realization that later poets and their critical followers tend to misread strong precursors by a fairly consistent mistaking of literal for figurative, and of figurative for literal. Browning misread the High Romantics, and particularly his prime precursor, Shelley, in this pattern, and through time's revenges most modern poets and critics have done and are doing the same to Browning. I am going to explore Browning, in this chapter, as the master of misprision he was, by attempting to show our tendency to read his epiphanies or "good moments" as ruinations or vastations of quest, and our parallel tendency to read his darkest visions-of-failure as if they were celebrations.

I will concentrate on a small group of Browning's poems including *Cleon, Master Hugues of Saxe-Gotha, A Toccata of Galuppi's, Abt Vogler,* and *Andrea del Sarto,* but I cannot evade for long my own obsession with *Childe Roland to the Dark Tower Came,* and so it and its contrary chant, *Thamuris Marching,* will enter late into this discourse. Indeed, I want to end with a kind of critical self-analysis, and ask myself the question: why am I obsessed by the *Childe Roland* poem, or rather, what does it *mean* to be obsessed by that poem? How is it that I cannot conceive of an antithetical practical criticism of poetry without constantly being compelled to use *Childe Roland* as a test case, as though it were the modern poem proper, more even than say, *Tintern Abbey* or *Byzantium* or *The Idea of Order at Key West?* Is there a way to make these questions center upon critical analysis rather than upon psychic self-analysis?

In Browning's prose *Essay on Shelley,* there is an eloquent passage that idealizes poetic influence:

> There is a time when the general eye has, so to speak, absorbed its fill of the phenomena around it, whether spiritual or material, and desires rather to learn the exacter significance of what it possesses, than to receive any augmentation of what is possessed. Then is the opportunity for the poet of loftier vision, to lift his fellows. . . . The influence of such an achievement will not soon die out. A tribe of successors

(Homerides) working more or less in the same spirit, dwell on his discoveries and reinforce his doctrine; till, at unawares, the world is found to be subsisting wholly on the shadow of a reality, on sentiments diluted from passions, on the tradition of a fact, the convention of a moral, the straw of last year's harvest.

Browning goes on to posit a mighty ladder of authentic poets, in an objective and subjective alternation, who will replace one another almost endlessly in succession, concerning which, "the world dares no longer doubt that its gradations ascend." Translated, this means: "Wordsworth to Shelley to Browning," in which Browning represents a triumph of what he calls the objective principle. Against Browning's prose idealization, I will set his attack upon the disciples of Keats in his poem *Popularity*:

> And there's the extract, flasked and fine,
>   And priced and saleable at last!
> And Hobbs, Nobbs, Stokes and Nokes combine
>   To paint the future from the past,
> Put blue into their line.

For "Hobbs, Nobbs, Stokes and Nokes" we might read Tennyson, Arnold, Rossetti, and whatever other contemporary Keatsian, whether voluntary or involuntary, that Browning wished to scorn. But the next stanza, the poem's last, would surely have cut against Browning himself if for "John Keats" we substituted "Percy Shelley":

> Hobbs hints blue,—straight he turtle eats:
>   Nobbs prints blue,—claret crowns his cup:
> Nokes outdares Stokes in azure feats,—
>   Both gorge. Who fished the murex up?
> What porridge had John Keats?

The vegetarian Shelley, according to his friend Byron, tended to dine on air and water, not fit fare for the strenuously hearty Browning, who in his later years was to become London's leading diner-out. But though Browning seems not to have had the slightest *personal* consciousness of an anxiety of influence, he wrote the most powerful poem ever to be explicitly concerned with the problem. This is the dramatic monologue *Cleon*, in which the imaginary jack-of-all-arts, Cleon, is in my judgment a kind of version of Matthew Arnold, whose *Empedocles on Etna* Browning had been reading. Arnold's Empedocles keeps lamenting his own and the world's belatedness, a lament that becomes a curious kind of inauthentic overconfidence in Cleon's self-defense:

> I have not chanted verse like Homer, no—
> Nor swept string like Terpander, no—nor carved
> And painted men like Phidias and his friend:
> I am not great as they are, point by point.
> But I have entered into sympathy
> With these four, running these into one soul,
> Who, separate, ignored each other's art.
> Say, is it nothing that I know them all?

Browning could enjoy the belatedness of Arnold or Rossetti, because no poet ever felt less belated than this exuberant daemon. We remember the malicious epithet applied to him by Hopkins: "Bouncing Browning." I think we can surmise that poetic belatedness as an affliction, whether conscious or unconscious, always rises in close alliance with ambivalence towards the prime precursor. Browning felt no ambivalence towards Shelley, such as Yeats had towards Shelley, or Shelley towards Wordsworth, or Wordsworth towards Milton. Browning loved Shelley unbrokenly and almost unreservedly from the age of fourteen, when he first read him, until his own death at the age of seventy-seven. But ambivalence is not the only matrix from which the anxiety of influence rises. There is perhaps a darker source in the guilt or shame of identifying the precursor with the ego-ideal, and then living on in the sense of having betrayed that identification by one's own failure to have become oneself, by a realization that the ephebe has betrayed his own integrity, and betrayed also the covenant that first bound him to the precursor. That guilt unmistakably was Browning's, as Betty Miller and others have shown, and so the burden of belatedness was replaced in Browning by a burden of dissimulation, a lying-against-the-self, rather than a lying-against-time.

But is not that kind of shame only another mask for the guilt-of-indebtedness, the only guilt that ever troubles a poet-as-poet? Certainly, Shelley for Browning was precisely the "numinous shadow" or ancestor-god whose baleful influence is stressed by Nietzsche. Rather than demonstrate this too obviously, whether by recourse to Browning's poem *Pauline* or by an examination of the unhappy episode in which the young Browning yielded to his stern mother's Evangelical will, I think it more interesting to seek out what is most difficult in Browning, which is the total contrast between his optimism, a quality both temperamental and theoretical, and the self-destructive peculiarities of his men and women. I want to start by puzzling over the grotesque and unique poem, *Master Hugues of Saxe-Gotha*, with its curious and central contrast between the charming organist who speaks the monologue and the heavy pseudo-Bachian composer, also invented by Browning, whose name is the poem's title. The relationship between performer and composer *is* the poem. This relationship is *not* a displaced form of the ambivalence between ephebe and precursor, because the performer's reading/misreading of the composer is very different from the later poet's interpretation of an earlier one, or anyone's reading/misreading of any poet. It is true that a performance is an interpretation, but a performance lacks the vital element of revisionism that makes for fresh creation. The charm of the poem *Master Hugues of Saxe-Gotha,* like the chill of the somewhat similar but greater poem, *A Toccata of Galuppi's,* is precisely that we are free of the burden of misprision and that the performer in each poem is more like a reciter of a text than he is like a critic of a text. Yet it remains true that you cannot recite any poem without giving some interpretation of it, though I would hazard the speculation that even the strongest recital, acting, or performance is at best a weak reading/misreading, in the technical antithetical senses of "weak" and "strong," for again there is no strength, poetic or critical, without the dialectics of revisionism coming into play.

The organist earnestly wants to understand Hugues without revising him, but evidently the world is right and the poor organist wrong, in that less is meant than meets the ear in Hugues' mountainous fugues. Hugues is a kind of involuntary musical nihilist, who in effect would rather have the void as purpose than be void of purpose. The organist is not only old-fashioned in his devotion to Hugues but, as we might say now, old-fashioned in his devotion to meaning. Yet skepticism, a suspicion concerning both meaning-in-Hugues and meaning-in-life, has begun to gain strength in the organist, despite himself. His quasi-desperate test-performance of Hugues, thematically racing the sacristan's putting-out of the light, moves from one sadly negative conclusion to a larger negation, from "But where's music, the dickens?" to:

> Is it your moral of Life?
>   Such a web, simple and subtle,
> Weave we on earth here in impotent strife,
>   Backward and forward each throwing his shuttle,
> Death ending all with a knife?

The very reluctance of the organist's interpretation convinces us of its relevance to Hugues. Hugues will not "say the word," despite the organist's plea, and the organist lacks the strength to break out on his revisionary own and do what he wants to do, which is "unstop the full-organ, / Blare out the *mode Palestrina,*" akin to the gentle simplicity of his own nature. Yet we must not take the organist too literally; after all, there is nothing whatsoever to prevent him from playing Palestrina to his own satisfaction in the moments of light that remain to him. But it is the problematical, cumbersome, absurdly intricate Hugues who obsesses him, whose secret or lack of a secret he is driven to solve. Despite himself, the organist is on an antithetical quest, like absolutely every other monologist in Browning. The luminous last line of the poem is to be answered, emphatically: "Yes!"

> While in the roof, if I'm right there,
> . . . Lo you, the wick in the socket!
> Hallo, you sacristan, show us a light there!
> Down it dips, gone like a rocket.
> What, you want, do you, to come unawares,
> Sweeping the church up for first morning-prayers,
> And find a poor devil has ended his cares
> At the foot of your rotten-runged rat-riddled stairs?
> Do I carry the moon in my pocket?

If the organist is right, then the gold in the gilt roof is a better emblem of a final reality than the spider web woven by Hugues. But fortunately the darkening of the light breaks in upon an uneasy affirmation, and leaves us instead with the realization that the organist is subject as well as object of his own quest for meaning. Hugues goes on weaving his intricate vacuities; the organist carries the moon in his pocket. Has the poem ended, however humorously, as a ruined quest or as a good moment? Does Browning make it possible for us to know the difference between the two? Or is it the particular achievement of his art that the difference cannot be known? Does the organist end by knowing he has been deceived, or does he end in the beautiful earliness of carrying imagination in his own pocket, in a transumptive allusion to the Second Spirit in one of Browning's favorite poems, Shelley's *The Two Spirits: An Allegory?* There the Second Spirit, overtly allegorizing desire, affirms that the "lamp of love," carried within, gives him the perpetual power to "make night day." Browning is more dialectical, and the final representation in his poem is deeply ambiguous. But that is a depth of repression that I want to stay with, and worry, for a space, if only because it bothers me that *Master Hugues of Saxe-Gotha,* like so many of Browning's poems, ends in an *aporia,* in the reader's uncertainty as to whether he is to read literally or figuratively. Browning personally, unlike Shelley, was anything but an intellectual skeptic, and that he should create figures that abide in our uncertainty is at once his most salient and his most challenging characteristic.

A *Toccata of Galuppi's* can be read as a reversal of this poem, since it appears to end in the performer's conscious admission of belatedness and defeat. But Browning was quite as multi-form a maker as poetic tradition affords, and the *Toccata* is as subtle a poem as ever he wrote. It invokes for us a grand Nietzschean question, from the Third Essay of *On the Genealogy of Morals:* "What does it mean when an artist leaps over into his opposite?" Nietzsche was thinking of Wagner, but Browning in the *Toccata* may be another instance. Nietzsche's ultimate answer to his own question prophesied late Freud, if we take the answer to be: "All great things bring about their own destruction through an act of self-overcoming." I think we can say rather safely that no one was less interested in *Selbstaufhebung* than Robert Browning; he was perfectly delighted to be at once subject and object of his own quest. Like Emerson, whom he resembles only in this single respect, he rejoiced always that there were so many of him, so many separate selves happily picnicking together in a single psyche. From a Nietzschean point of view, he must seem only an epitome of some of the most outrageous qualities of the British empirical and Evangelical minds, but he is actually more sublimely outrageous even than that. There are no dialectics that can subsume him, because he is not so much evasive as he is preternatural, wholly daemonic, with an astonishing alliance perpetual in him between an impish cunning and endless linguistic energy. I think we can surmise why he was so fascinated by poets like Christopher Smart and Thomas Lovell Beddoes, poets who represented the tradition of Dissenting Enthusiasm carried over into actual madness. With energies like Browning's, and self-confidence like Browning's, it took a mind as powerful as Browning's to avoid being carried by Enthusiasm into alienation, but perhaps the oddest of all Browning's endless oddities is that he was incurably sane, even as he imagined his gallery of pathological enthusiasts, monomaniacs, and marvelous charlatans.

There are at least four voices coldly leaping along in A *Toccata of Galuppi's,* and only one of them is more or less Browning's, and we cannot be certain even of that. Let us break in for the poem's conclusion, as the monologist first addresses the composer whose "touch-piece" he is playing, and next the composer answers back, *but only through the monologist's performance,* and finally the speaker-performer acknowledges his defeat by the heartlessly brilliant Galuppi:

[Stanzas XI–XV have been deleted from text.]

The "swerve" *is* the Lucretian *clinamen,* and we might say that Galuppi, like Lucretius, assaults the monologist-performer with the full strength of the Epicurean argument. One possible interpretation is that

Browning, as a fierce Transcendentalist of his own sect, a sect of one, is hammering at the Victorian spiritual compromise, which his cultivated speaker exemplifies. That interpretation would confirm the poem's serio-comic opening:

> Oh Galuppi, Baldassaro, this is very sad to find!
> I can hardly misconceive you; it would prove me deaf and blind;
> But although I take your meaning, 'tis with such a heavy mind!

Galuppi's triumph, on this reading, would be the dramatic one of shaking up this cultivated monologist, who first half-scoffs at Galuppi's nihilism, but who ends genuinely frightened by the lesson Galuppi has taught which is a lesson of mortality and consequent meaninglessness. But I think that is to underestimate the monologist, who is a more considerable temperament even than the organist who plays Hugues and can bear neither to give Hugues up nor accept Hugues' emptiness. Galuppi is no Hugues, but a powerfully sophisticated artist who gives what was wanted of him, but with a Dance-of-Death aspect playing against his audience's desires. And the speaker, who knows physics, some geology, a little mathematics, and will not quite abandon his Christian immortality, is at least as enigmatic as the organist, and for a parallel reason. Why cannot he let Galuppi alone? What does he quest for in seeing how well he can perform that spirited and elegant art? Far more even than Galuppi, or Galuppi's audience, or than Browning, the speaker is obsessed with mortality:

> Then they left you for their pleasure: till in due time, one by one,
> Some with lives that came to nothing, some with deeds as well undone,
> Death stepped tacitly and took them where they never see the sun.

One of the most moving elements in the poem is its erotic nostalgia, undoubtedly the single sphere of identity between the monologist and Browning himself. Eros crowds the poem, with an intensity and poignance almost Shakespearean in its strength. Nothing in the poem is at once so moving and so shocking as the monologist's final "Dear dead women, with such hair, too—," for this spiritual trimmer is very much a sensual man, like his robust creator. It is the cold Galuppi who is more the dualist, more the artist fulfilling the Nietzschean insight that the ascetic ideal is a defensive evasion by which art preserves itself against the truth. But where, as readers, does that leave us, since this time Browning elegantly has cleared himself away? His overt intention is pretty clear, and I think pretty irrelevant also. He wants us—unlike the monologist, unlike Galuppi, unlike Galuppi's hard-living men and women—to resort to his ferocious version of an antithetical Protestantism, which is I think ultimately his misprision of Shelley's antithetical humanism. Yet Browning's art has freed us of Browning, though paradoxically not of Shelley, or at least of the strong Lucretian element in Shelley. Has the monologist quested after Galuppi's truth, only to end up in a vastation of his own comforting evasions of the truth? That would be the canonical reading, but it would overliteralize a metaleptic figuration that knowingly has chosen not to attempt a reversal of time. When the speaker ends by feeling "chilly and grown old," then he has introjected Galuppi's world and Galuppi's music, and projected his own compromise formulations. But this is an *illusio*, a metaleptic figuration that is on the verge of becoming an opening irony or reaction-formation again, that is, rejoining the tone of jocular evasion that began the poem. Nothing has happened because nothing has changed, and the final grimness of Browning's eerie poem is that its speaker is caught in a repetition. He will pause awhile, and then play a toccata of Galuppi's again.

Let us try a third music-poem or improvisation, the still more formidable *Abt Vogler*, where the daemonic performer is also the momentary composer, inventing fitfully upon an instrument of his own invention, grandly solitary because there is nothing for him to interpret except his own interpretation of his own creation. The canonical readings available here are too weak to be interesting, since they actually represent the poem as being pious. The historical Vogler was regarded by some as a pious fraud, but Browning's Vogler is too complex to be regarded either as an impostor or as sincerely devout. What matters most is that he is primarily an extemporizer, rather than necessarily an artist, whether as performer or composer. The poem leaves open (whatever Browning's intentions) the problem of whether Vogler is a skilled illusionist, or something more than that. At the least, Vogler is self-deceived, but even the self-deception is most complex. It is worth knowing what I must assume that Browning knew: Vogler's self-invented instruments sounded splendid only when played by Vogler. Though the great temptation in reading this poem is to interpret it as a good moment precariously attained, and then lost, I think the stronger or antithetical reading here will show that this is very nearly as much a poem of ruined quest as *Childe Roland* or *Andrea del Sarto* is.

Abt Vogler is one of those poems that explain Yeats's remark to the effect that he feared Browning as a potentially dangerous influence upon him. If we could read *Abt Vogler* without interpretative suspicion (and I believe we cannot), then the poem would seem to be a way-station between the closing third of *Adonais* and Yeats's Byzantium poems. It establishes itself in a state of being that seems either to be beyond the antithesis of life and death, or else that seems to be the state of art itself. Yet, in the poem *Abt Vogler,* I think we have neither, but something more puzzling, a willed phantasmagoria that is partly Browning's and partly an oddity, a purely visionary dramatic monologue.

Vogler, we ought to realize immediately, does not seek the purposes of art, which after all is hard work. Vogler is daydreaming, and is seeking a magical power over nature or supernature, as in the debased Kabbalist myth of Solomon's seal. Vogler is not so much playing his organ as enslaving it to his magical purposes, purposes that do not distinguish between angel and demon, heaven and hell. Vogler is no Blakean visionary; he seeks not to marry heaven and hell, but merely to achieve every power that he can. And yet he has a moving purpose, akin to Shelley's in *Prometheus Unbound,* which is to aid earth's mounting into heaven. But, is his vision proper something we can grant the prestige of vision, or is there not a dubious element in it?

Being made perfect, when the subject is someone like Vogler, is a somewhat chancy phenomenon. Unlike the sublimely crazy Johannes Agricola, in one of Browning's earliest and most frightening dramatic monologues, Vogler is not a genuine Enthusiast, certain of his own Election. Stanza VI has a touch of *Cleon* about it, and stanza VII is clearly *unheimlich,* despite the miraculous line: "That out of three sounds he frame, not a fourth sound, but a star." But with stanzas VIII and IX, which are this poem's *askesis* or sublimation, it is not so easy to distinguish Vogler from Browning, or one of the beings always bouncing around in Browning, anyway:

VIII

Well, it is gone at last, the palace of music I reared;
    Gone! and the good tears start, the praises that come too slow;
For one is assured at first, one scarce can say that he feared,
    That he even gave it a thought, the gone thing was to go.
Never to be again! But many more of the kind
    As good, nay, better perchance: is this your comfort to me?
To me, who must be saved because I cling with my mind
    To the same, same self, same love, same God: ay, what was, shall be.

IX

Therefore to whom turn I but to thee, the ineffable Name?
    Builder and maker, thou, of houses not made with hands!

> What, have fear of change from thee who art ever the same?
>> Doubt that thy power can fill the heart that thy power expands?
> There shall never be one lost good! What was, shall live as before;
>> The evil is null, is nought, is silence implying sound;
> What was good shall be good, with, for evil, so much good more;
>> On the earth the broken arcs; in the heaven, a perfect round.

The poem, from here to the end, in the three final stanzas, is suddenly as much Browning's Magnificat as the *Song to David*, which is deliberately echoed in the penultimate line, is Smart's. But what does that mean, whether in this poem, or whether about Browning himself? Surely he would not acknowledge, openly, that his is the art of the extemporizer, the illusionist improvising? Probably not, but the poem may be acknowledging an anxiety that he possesses, to much that effect. Whether this is so or not, to any degree, how are we to read the final stanza?

> Well, it is earth with me; silence resumes her reign:
>> I will be patient and proud, and soberly acquiesce.
> Give me the keys. I feel for the common chord again,
>> Sliding by semitones, till I sink to the minor,—yes,
> And I blunt it into a ninth, and I stand on alien ground,
>> Surveying awhile the heights I rolled from into the deep;
> Which, hark, I have dared and done, for my resting-place is found,
>> The C Major of this life: so now I will try to sleep.

This descent to C Major separates Vogler totally from Browning again, since of the many keys in which the genuinely musical Browning composes, his resting place is hardly a key without sharps or flats. Browning has his direct imitation of Smart's *Song to David* in his own overtly religious poem, *Saul*, and so we can be reasonably certain that Vogler does not speak for Browning when the improviser belatedly stands on alien ground, surveying the Sublime he had attained, and echoes Smart's final lines:

> Thou at stupendous truth believ'd;—
> And now the matchless deed's achiev'd,
>> DETERMINED, DARED, and DONE.

What Vogler has dared and done is no more than to have dreamed a belated dream; where Browning is, in regard to that Promethean or Shelleyan a dream, is an enigma, at least in this poem. What *Abt Vogler*, as a text, appears to proclaim *is* the impossibility of our reading it, insofar as reading means being able to govern the interplay of literal and figurative meanings in a text. Canonically, in terms of all received readings, this poem is almost an apocalyptic version of a Browningesque "Good

Moment," a time of privilege or an epiphany, a sudden manifestation of highest vision. Yet the patterns of revisionary misprision are clearly marked upon the poem, and they tend to indicate that the poem demands to be read figuratively against its own letter, as another parable of ruined quest, or confession or imaginative failure, or the shame of knowing such failure.

I turn to *Andrea del Sarto,* which with *Childe Roland to the Dark Tower Came,* and the meditation entitled *The Pope* in *The Ring and the Book,* seems to me to represent Browning at his greatest. Here there would appear to be no question about the main issue of interpretation, for the canonical readings seem fairly close to the poem in its proclamation that this artist's quest is ruined, that Andrea stands self-condemned by his own monologue. Betty Miller has juxtaposed the poem, brilliantly, with this troubled and troublesome passage in Browning's *Essay on Shelley:*

> Although of such depths of failure there can be no question here we must in every case betake ourselves to the review of a poet's life ere we determine some of the nicer questions concerning his poetry,—more especially if the performance we seek to estimate aright, has been obstructed and cut short of completion by circumstances,—a disastrous youth or a premature death. We may learn from the biography whether his spirit invariably saw and spoke from the last height to which it had attained. An absolute vision is not for this world, but we are permitted a continual approximation to it, every degree of which in the individual, provided it exceed the attainment of the masses, must procure him a clear advantage. Did the poet ever attain to a higher platform than where he rested and exhibited a result? Did he know more than he spoke of?

On this juxtaposition, Andrea and Browning alike rested on a level lower than the more absolute vision they could have attained. Certainly Andrea tells us, perhaps even shows us, that he knows more than he paints. But Browning? If he was no Shelley, he was also no Andrea, which in part is the burden of the poem. But only in part, and whether there is some level of *apologia* in this monologue, in its patterning, rather than its overt content, is presumably a question that a more antithetical practical criticism ought to be capable of exploring.

Does Andrea overrate his own potential? If he does, *then there is no poem,* for unless his dubious gain-in-life has paid for a genuine loss-in-art, then he is too self-deceived to be interesting, even to himself. Browning has complicated this matter, as he complicates everything. The poem's subtitle reminds us that Andrea was called "The Faultless Painter," and Vasari, Browning's source, credits Andrea with everything in execution but then faults him for lacking ambition, for not attempting the Sublime.

Andrea, in the poem, persuades us of a wasted greatness not so much by his boasting ("At any rate 'tis easy, all of it! / No sketches first, no studies, that's long past: / I do what many dream of, all their lives . . ."), but by his frightening skill in sketching his own twilight-piece, by his showing us how "A common greyness silvers everything—." Clearly, this speaker knows loss, and clearly he is the antithesis of his uncanny creator, whose poetry never suffers from a lack of ambition, who is always Sublime where he is most Grotesque, and always Grotesque when he storms the Sublime. Andrea does not represent anything in Browning directly, not even the betrayed relationship of the heroic precursor, yet he does represent one of Browning's anxieties, an anxiety related to but not identical with the anxiety of influence. It is an anxiety of representation, or a fear of forbidden meanings, or in Freudian language precisely a fear of the return-of-the-repressed, even though such a return would cancel out a poem-as-poem, or is it *because* such a return would end poetry as such?

Recall that Freud's notion of repression speaks of an unconsciously *purposeful* forgetting, and remind yourself also that what Browning could never bear was a sense of *purposelessness*. It is purposelessness that haunts Childe Roland, and we remember again what may be Nietzsche's most powerful insight, which closes the great Third Essay of On the Genealogy of Morals. The ascetic ideal, Nietzsche said, by which he meant also the aesthetic ideal, was the only *meaning* yet found for human suffering, and mankind would rather have the void *for* purpose than be void *of* purpose. Browning's great fear, purposelessness, was related to the single quality that had moved and impressed him most in Shelley: the remorseless purposefulness of the Poet in *Alastor*, of Prometheus, and of Shelley himself questing for death in *Adonais*. Andrea, as an artist, is the absolute antithesis of the absolute idealist Shelley, and so Andrea is a representation of profound Browningesque anxiety.

But how is this an anxiety of representation? We enter again the dubious area of *belatedness*, which Browning is reluctant to represent, but is too strong and authentic a poet to avoid. Though Andrea uses another vocabulary, a defensively evasive one, to express his relationship to Michelangelo, Raphael, and Leonardo, he suffers the burden of the latecomer. His Lucrezia is the emblem of his belatedness, his planned excuse for his failure in strength, which he accurately diagnoses as a failure in will. And he ends in deliberate belatedness, and in his perverse need to be cuckolded:

> What would one have?
> In heaven, perhaps, new chances, one more chance—
> Four great walls in the New Jerusalem,
> Meted on each side by the angel's reed,

For Leonard, Rafael, Agnolo and me
To cover—the three first without a wife,
While I have mine! So—still they overcome
Because there's still Lucrezia,—as I choose.
Again the Cousin's whistle! Go, my Love.

Can we say that Andrea represents what Shelley dreaded to become, the extinguished hearth, an ash without embers? We know that Shelley need not have feared, yet the obsessive, hidden fear remains impressive. Browning at seventy-seven was as little burned out as Hardy at eighty-eight, Yeats at seventy-four, or Stevens at seventy-five, and his *Asolando,* his last book, fiercely prefigures Hardy's *Winter Words,* Yeats's *Last Poems,* and Stevens's *The Rock,* four astonishing last bursts of vitalism in four of the strongest modern poets. What allies the four volumes (*The Rock* is actually the last section of Stevens's *Collected Poems,* but he had planned it as a separate volume under the title *Autumn Umber*) is their overcoming of each poet's abiding anxiety of representation. "Representation," in poetry, ultimately means self-advocacy; as Hartman says: "You justify either the self or that which stands greatly against it: perhaps both at once." We could cite Nietzsche here on the poet's Will-to-Power, but the more orthodox Coleridge suffices, by reminding us that there can be no origination without discontinuity, and that only the Will can interrupt the repetition-compulsion that *is* nature. In the final phases of Browning, Hardy, Yeats, and Stevens, the poet's Will raises itself against Nature, and this antithetical spirit breaks through a final anxiety and dares to represent itself as what Coleridge called self-determining spirit. Whether Freud would have compounded this self-realizing instinct with his "detours towards death" I do not know, but I think it is probable. In this final phase, Browning and his followers (Hardy and Yeats were overtly influenced by Browning, and I would suggest a link between the extemporizing, improvising aspect of Stevens, and Browning) are substituting a transumptive representation for the still-abiding presence of Shelley, their common ancestor.

I want to illustrate this difficult point by reference to Browning's last book, particularly to its *Prologue,* and to the sequence called *Bad Dreams.* My model, ultimately, is again the Lurianic Kabbalah, with its notion of *gilgul,* of lifting up a precursor's spark, provided that he is truly one's precursor, truly of one's own root. *Gilgul* is the ultimate *tikkun,* as far as an act of representation can go. What Browning does is fascinatingly like the pattern of *gilgul,* for at the end he takes up precisely Shelley's dispute with Shelley's prime precursor, Wordsworth. By doing for Shelley what Shelley could not do for himself, overcome Wordsworth, Browning lifts up or redeems Shelley's spark or ember, and renews the power celebrated in the *Ode to the West Wind* and Act IV of *Prometheus Unbound*. I will try to illustrate this complex pattern, after these glances at *Asolando*, by returning for a last time (I hope) to my personal obsession with *Childe Roland to the Dark Tower Came*, and then concluding this discourse by considering Browning's late reversal of *Childe Roland* in the highly Shelleyan celebration, *Thamuris Marching*.

The *Prologue* to *Asolando* is another in that long series of revisions of the *Intimations* Ode that form so large a part of the history of nineteenth- and twentieth-century British and American poetry. But Browning con- sciously gives a revision of a revision, compounding *Alastor* and the *Hymn to Intellectual Beauty* with the parent poem. What counts in Browning's poem is not the Wordsworthian gleam, called here, in the first stanza, an "alien glow," but the far more vivid Shelleyan fire, that Browning recalls seeing for the first time, some fifty years before:

> How many a year, my Asolo,
>   Since—one step just from sea to land—
> I found you, loved yet feared you so—
>   For natural objects seemed to stand
> Palpably fire-clothed! No—
>
> No mastery of mine o'er these!
>   Terror with beauty, like the Bush
> Burning but unconsumed. Bend knees,
>   Drop eyes to earthward! Language? Tush!
> Silence 'tis awe decrees.
>
> And now? The lambent flame is—where?
>   Lost from the naked world: earth, sky,
> Hill, vale, tree, flower,—Italia's rare
>   O'er-running beauty crowds the eye—
> But flame? The Bush is bare.

When Shelley abandoned the fire, then it was for the transumptive trumpet of a prophecy, or in *Adonais* for the same wind rising ("The breath whose might I have invoked in song / Descends on me") to carry him beyond voice as beyond sight. Browning, as an Evangelical Protes- tant, fuses the Shelleyan heritage with the Protestant God in a powerfully incongruous transumption:

> Hill, vale, tree, flower—they stand distinct,
>   Nature to know and name. What then?
> A Voice spoke thence which straight unlinked
>   Fancy from fact: see, all's in ken:
> Has once my eyelid winked?

No, for the purged ear apprehends
    Earth's import, not the eye late dazed:
The voice said 'Call my works thy friends!
    At Nature dost thou shrink amazed?
God is it who transcends.'

This is an absolute logocentrism, and is almost more than any poem can bear, particularly at a time as late as 1889. Browning gets away with it partly by way of a purged ear, partly because his Protestantism condenses what High Romanticism normally displaces, the double-bind situation of the Protestant believer whose God simultaneously says "Be Like Me in My stance towards Nature" and "Do not presume to resemble Me in My stance towards nature." The sheer energy of the Browningesque demonic Sublime carries the poet past what ought to render him imaginatively schizoid.

But not for long, of course, as a glance at *Bad Dreams* will indicate, a glance that then will take us back to the greatest of Browning's nightmares, the demonic romance of *Childe Roland. Bad Dreams III* is a poem in which the opposition between Nature and Art *has* been turned into a double-bind, with its contradictory injunctions:

This was my dream! I saw a Forest
    Old as the earth, no track nor trace
Of unmade man. Thou, Soul, explorest—
    Though in a trembling rapture—space
Immeasurable! Shrubs, turned trees,
Trees that touch heaven, support its frieze
Studded with sun and moon and star:
While—oh, the enormous growths that bar
Mine eye from penetrating past
    Their tangled twine where lurks—nay, lives
Royally lone, some brute-type cast
    In the rough, time cancels, man forgives.

On, Soul! I saw a lucid City
    Of architectural device
Every way perfect. Pause for pity,
    Lightning! Nor leave a cicatrice
On those bright marbles, dome and spire,
Structures palatial,—streets which mire
Dares not defile, paved all too fine
For human footstep's smirch, not thine—
Proud solitary traverser,
    My Soul, of silent lengths of way—
With what ecstatic dread, aver,
    Lest life start sanctioned by thy stay!

Ah, but the last sight was the hideous!
    A city, yes,—a Forest, true,—

But each devouring each. Perfidious
    Snake-plants had strangled what I knew
Was a pavilion once: each oak
Held on his horns some spoil he broke
By surreptitiously beneath
Upthrusting: pavements, as with teeth,
Griped huge weed widening crack and split
    In squares and circles stone-work erst.
Oh, Nature—good! Oh, Art—no whit
    Less worthy! Both in one—accurst!

In the sequence of *Bad Dreams*, Browning himself, as interpreter of his own text, identifies Nature with the husband, Art with the wife, and the marriage of Art and Nature, man and woman—why, with Hell, and a sadomasochistic sexual Hell, at that. But the text can sustain very diverse interpretations, as the defensive intensity of repression here is enormously strong. The City is of Art, but like Yeats's Byzantium, which it prophesies, it is also a City of Death-in-Life, and the previous vision of the forest is one of a Nature that might be called Life-in-Death. Neither realm can bear the other, in both senses of "bear"—"bring forth" or "tolerate." Neither is the other's precursor, and each devours the other, if they are brought together. This is hardly the vision of the *Prologue* to *Asolando*, as there seems no room for either Browning or God in the world of the final stanza. Granted that this is nightmare, or severe repression partly making a return, it carries us back to Browning at his most problematic and Sublime, to his inverted vision of the Center, *Childe Roland to the Dark Tower Came*.

As the author of two full-scale commentaries on this poem (in *The Ringers in the Tower*, 1971, and in *A Map of Misreading*, 1975) I reapproach the text with considerable wariness, fairly determined not only that I will not repeat myself, but also hopefully aiming not merely to uncover my own obsessional fixation upon so grandly grotesque a quest-romance. But I recur to the question I asked at the start of this discourse; is there an attainable *critical* knowledge to be gathered from this critical obsession?

Roland, though a Childe or ephebe on the road to a demonic version of the Scene of Instruction, is so consciously belated a quester that he seems at least as much an obsessive interpreter as anything else purposive that he might desire to become. He out-Nietzsches Nietzsche's Zarathustra in his compulsive will-to-power over the interpretation of his own text. It is difficult to conceive of a more belated hero, and I know of no more extreme literary instance of a quest emptying itself out. Borges accurately located in Browning one of the precursors of Kafka, and perhaps only Kafka's *The Castle* rivals *Childe Roland* as a Gnostic version of what was once romance. Nearly every figuration in the poem reduces to ruin, yet the poem, as all of us obscurely sense, appears to end in something like triumph, in a Good Moment carried through to a supreme representation:

> There they stood, ranged along the hill-sides, met
>> To view the last of me, a living frame
>> For one more picture! in a sheet of flame
> I saw them and I knew them all. And yet
> Dauntless the slug-horn to my lips I set,
>> And blew, *'Childe Roland to the Dark Tower came.'*

Surely it is outrageous to call this a Supreme or even a Good Moment? The stanza just before ends with the sound of loss: "one moment knelled the woe of years." Wordsworth and Coleridge had viewed the Imagination as compensatory, as trading off experiential loss for poetic gain, a formula that we can begin to believe was an unmitigated calamity. It is the peculiar fascination of *Childe Roland,* as a poem, that it undoes every High Romantic formula, that it exposes the Romantic imagination as being merely an accumulative principle of repression. But such negation is itself simplistic, and evades what is deepest and most abiding in this poem, which is the representation of *power*. For here, I think, is the kernel of our critical quest, that Kabbalistic point which is at once *ayin,* or nothingness, and *ehyeh,* or the representation of Absolute Being, the rhetorical irony or *illusio* that always permits a belated poem to begin again in its quest for renewed strength. Signification has wandered away, and Roland is questing for lost and forgotten *meaning,* questing for *representation,* for a seconding or re-advocacy of his own self. Does he not succeed, far better than Tennyson's Ulysses and Percivale, and far better even than the Solitaries of the High Romantics, in this quest for representation? Let us grant him, and ourselves, that this is a substitute for his truly impossible original objective, for that was the *antithetical,* Shelleyan dream of rebegetting oneself, of breaking through the web of nature and so becoming one's own imaginative father. Substitution, as Roland shows, needs not be a sublimation, but can move from repression *through* sublimation to climax in a more complex act of defense.

Psychoanalysis has no single name for this act, unless we were willing (as we are not) to accept the pejorative one of paranoia for what is, from any point of view that transcends the analytic, a superbly valuable act of the will. Roland teaches us that what psychoanalysis calls "introjection" and "projection" are figurations for the spiritual processes of identification and apocalyptic rejection that exist at the outer borders of poetry. Roland learns, and we learn with him, that the representation of power *is* itself a power, and that this latter power or strength is the only purposiveness that we shall know. Roland, at the close, is re-inventing the self, but at the considerable expense of joining that self to a visionary company of loss, and loss means loss of *meaning* here. The endless fascination of his poem, for any critical reader nurtured upon Romantic tradition, is that the poem, more clearly than any other, nevertheless does precisely what any strong Romantic poem does, at once de-idealizes itself far more thoroughly than we can de-idealize it, yet points also beyond this self-deconstruction or limitation or reduction to the First Idea, on to a re-imagining, to a power-making that no other discursive mode affords. For Roland, as persuasively as any fictive being, warns us against the poisonous ravishments of truth itself. He and his reader have moved only through discourse together, and he and his reader are less certain about what they know than they were as the poem began, but both he and his reader have endured unto a representation of more strength than they had at the start, and such a representation indeed turns out to be a kind of restitution, a *tikkun* for repairing a fresh breaking-of-the-vessels. Meaning has been more curtailed than restored, but strength is revealed as antithetical to meaning.

I conclude with a great poem by Browning that is his conscious revision of *Childe Roland:* the marvelous late chant, *Thamuris Marching,* which is one of the finest unknown, unread poems by a major poet in the language. Twenty-two years after composing *Childe Roland,* Browning, not at the problematic age of thirty-nine, but now sixty-one, knows well that no spring has followed or flowered past meridian. But *Childe Roland* is a belated poem, except in its transumptive close, while all of *Thamuris Marching* accomplishes a metaleptic reversal, for how could a poem be more overwhelmingly early than this? And yet the situation of the quester is objectively terrible from the start of this poem, for Thamuris *knows* he is marching to an unequal contest, a poetic struggle of one heroic ephebe against the greatest of precursors, the Muses themselves. "Thamuris marching," the strong phrase repeated three times in the chant, expresses the *exuberance of purpose,* the Shelleyan remorseless joy in pure, self-destructive poetic quest, that Browning finally is able to grant himself.

Here is Browning's source, *Iliad* II, 594 ff:

> . . . and Dorion, where the Muses
> encountering Thamyris the Thracian stopped him from
> singing, as he came from Oichalia and Oichalian Eurytos;
> for he boasted that he would surpass, if the very Muses,

daughters of Zeus who holds the aegis, were singing against him.
and these in their anger struck him maimed, and the voice of wonder
they took away, and made him a singer without memory;

(Lattimore version)

Homer does not say that Thamyris lost the contest, but rather that
the infuriated Muses lost their divine temper, and unvoiced him by
maiming his memory, without which no one can be a poet. Other sources,
presumably known to Browning, mention a contest decided in the Muses'
favor by Apollo, after which those ungracious ladies blinded Thamyris,
and removed his memory, so as to punish him for his presumption.
Milton, in the invocation to light that opens Book III of *Paradise Lost*,
exalted Thamyris by coupling him with Homer, and then associated his
own ambitions with both poets:

Nightly I visit: nor sometimes forget
Those other two equall'd with me in Fate,
So were I equall'd with them in renown,
Blind Thamyris and blind Maemonides.

Milton presumably had read in Plutarch that Thamyris was cred-
ited with an epic about the war waged by the Titans against the Gods, the
theme that Browning would associate with Shelley and with Keats. Browning's Thamuris marches to a Shelleyan *terza rima*, and marches through a
visionary universe distinctly like Shelley's, and overtly proclaimed as
being *early*: "From triumph on to triumph, mid a ray / Of early morn—."
Laughing as he goes, yet knowing fully his own doom, Thamuris marches
through a landscape of joy that is the deliberate point-by-point reversal of
Childe Roland's self-made phantasmagoria of ordeal-by-landscape:

Thamuris, marching, laughed 'Each flake of foam'
(As sparklingly the ripple raced him by)
'Mocks slower clouds adrift in the blue dome!'

For Autumn was the season; red the sky
Held morn's conclusive signet of the sun
To break the mists up, bid them blaze and die.

Morn had the mastery as, one by one
All pomps produced themselves along the tract
From earth's far ending to near Heaven begun.

Was there a ravaged tree? it laughed compact
With gold, a leaf-ball crisp, high-brandished now,
Tempting to onset frost which late attacked.

Was there a wizened shrub, a starveling bough,
A fleecy thistle filched from by the wind,
A weed, Pan's trampling hoof would disallow?

> Each, with a glory and a rapture twined
> About it, joined the rush of air and light
> And force: the world was of one joyous mind.
> $\qquad\qquad\qquad\qquad\qquad\qquad$ (19–36)

From Roland's reductive interpretations we have passed to the imagination's heightened expansions. And though this quest is necessarily for the fearful opposite of poetic divination, we confront, not ruin, but the Good Moment exalted and transfigured, as though for once Browning utterly could fuse literal and figurative:

> Say not the birds flew! they forebore their right—
> Swam, reveling onward in the roll of things.
> Say not the beasts' mirth bounded! that was flight—
>
> How could the creatures leap, no lift of wings?
> Such earth's community of purpose, such
> The ease of earth's fulfilled imaginings—
>
> So did the near and far appear to touch
> In the moment's transport—that an interchange
> Of function, far with near, seemed scarce too much;
> $\qquad\qquad\qquad\qquad\qquad\qquad$ (37–45)

Roland's band of failures has become the glorious band of precursors among whom Thamuris predominates. The Shelleyan west wind of imagination rises, Destroyer and Creater, as Thamuris, eternally early, stands as the true ephebe, "Earth's poet," against the Heavenly Muse:

> Therefore the morn-ray that enriched his face,
> If it gave lambent chill, took flame again
> From flush of pride; he saw, he knew the place.
>
> What wind arrived with all the rhythms from plain,
> Hill, dale, and that rough wildwood interspersed?
> Compounding these to one consummate strain,
>
> It reached him, music; but his own outburst
> Of victory concluded the account,
> And that grew song which was mere music erst.
>
> 'Be my Parnassos, thou Pangaian mount!
> And turn thee, river, nameless hitherto!
> Famed shalt thou vie with famed Pieria's fount!
>
> 'Here I await the end of this ado:
> Which wins—Earth's poet or the Heavenly Muse.'

There is the true triumph of Browning's art, for the ever-early Thamuris is Browning as he wished to have been, locked in a solitary struggle against the precursor-principle, but struggling *in* the visionary

world of the precursor. Roland rode through a Gnostic universe in which
the hidden God, Shelley, was repressed, a repression that gave Browning a
negative triumph of the Sublime made Grotesque. In *Thamuris Marching*,
the joyous struggle is joined overtly, and the repressed partly returns, to be
repressed again into the true Sublime, as Browning lifts up the sparks of
his own root, to invoke that great mixed metaphor of the Lurianic
Kabbalah. There is a breaking-of-the-vessels, but the sparks are scattered
again, and become Shelley's *and* Browning's words, mixed together, among
mankind.

ROBERT LANGBAUM

The Dramatic Monologue: Sympathy versus Judgment

W riters on the dramatic monologue never fail to remark how little has been written on the subject—and I shall be no exception. The reason for the neglect is, I think, that no one has quite known what to do with the dramatic monologue except to classify it, to distinguish kinds of dramatic monologues and to distinguish the dramatic monologue from both the lyrical and the dramatic or narrative genres. Such classifications are all too easily made and have a way of killing off further interest in the subject. For they too often mean little beyond themselves, they close doors where they ought to open them.

The usual procedure in discussing the dramatic monologue is to find precedents for the form in the poetry of all periods, and then to establish, on the model of a handful of poems by Browning and Tennyson, objective criteria by which the form is henceforth to be recognized and judged. The procedure combines, I think, opposite mistakes; it is at once too restrictive and not restrictive enough, and in either case tells us too little. For once we decide to treat the dramatic monologue as a traditional genre, then every lyric in which the speaker seems to be someone other than the poet, almost all love-songs and laments in fact (*Lycidas, The Song of Songs, Polyphemus' Complaint* by Theocritus, the Anglo-Saxon *Banished Wife's Complaint*) become dramatic monologues; as do all imaginary epistles and orations and all kinds of excerpts from plays and narratives—e.g. all long speeches and soliloquies, those portions of epics in which the hero

From *The Poetry of Experience: The Dramatic Monologue in Modern Literary Tradition.* Copyright © 1957 by Robert Langbaum.

recounts the events that occurred before the opening of the poem, Chaucer's prologues to the *Canterbury Tales* and the tales themselves since they are told by fictitious persons: almost all first person narratives, in fact, become dramatic monologues. While such a classification is *true* enough, what does it accomplish except to identify a certain mechanical resemblance? —since the poems retain more affinity to the lyric, the drama, the narrative than to each other.

But if we are, on the other hand, too restrictive, we do little more than describe the handful of Browning and Tennyson poems we are using as models. We come out with the idea that dramatic monologues are more or less like Browning's *My Last Duchess*, and that most dramatic monologues being rather less like it are not nearly so good. We are told, for example, that the dramatic monologue must have not only a speaker other than the poet but also a listener, an occasion, and some interplay between speaker and listener. But since a classification of this sort does not even cover all the dramatic monologues of Browning and Tennyson, let alone those of other poets, it inevitably leads to quarrels about which poems are to be admitted into the canon; and worse, it leads to sub-classifications, to a distinction between what one writer calls "formal" dramatic monologues, which have only three of the necessary criteria, and "typical" dramatic monologues, which have all four. As for poems with only the dramatized speaker and perhaps the occasion—poems like Tennyson's *St Simeon Stylites* and Browning's *Childe Roland* and *Caliban,* which are among the best and most famous of all dramatic monologues—this writer, in order to salvage her classification, calls them "approximations."

The trouble with so narrow a criterion is that it suggests a decline of the dramatic monologue since Browning's time. It blinds us to the developing life of the form, to the importance of dramatic monologues in the work of such twentieth-century poets as Yeats, Eliot, Pound, Frost, Masters, Robinson and both Lowells, Amy and Robert (the form is particularly favoured by American poets). Robert Lowell's latest volume (*The Mills of the Kavanaughs*, 1951) consists entirely of dramatic monologues; while Pound, who in many places acknowledges his debt to Browning, has said of the dramatic monologues of Browning's *Men and Women* that "the form of these poems is the most vital form of that period," and has called a volume of his own *Personae.* Although Eliot has little to say in favour of Browning, the dramatic monologue has been the main form in his work until he assumed what appears to be a personal voice in the series of religious meditations beginning with *Ash Wednesday.* The dramatic monologue is proportionately as important in Eliot's work as in Browning's, Eliot having contributed more to the development of the form than any poet since Browning. Certainly *Prufrock, Portrait of a Lady, Gerontion, Journey of the Magi, A Song for Simeon* and *Marina* do as much credit to the dramatic monologue as anything of Browning's; while in *The Waste Land* Eliot has opened new possibilities for the form by constructing a kind of *collage* of dramatic monologues as perceived by Tiresias, whose dramatic monologue the poem is.

To understand the continuing life of the dramatic monologue, we must abandon the exclusive concern with objective criteria by which poems are either combined when they lack any effect in common, or else are separated when they have a common effect but lack the necessary mechanical resemblance. It is when we look inside the dramatic monologue, when we consider its effect, its *way* of meaning, that we see its connection with the poetry that precedes and follows Browning. We see, on the one hand, that the dramatic monologue is unprecedented in its effect, that its effect distinguishes it, in spite of mechanical resemblance, from the monologues of traditional poetry; and on the other hand, we welcome as particularly illuminating just those "approximations" that distress the classifiers. We welcome them because, having without the mechanical resemblance the same effect as the so-called "typical" dramatic monologues, they show us what the form is essentially doing.

One writer on the dramatic monologue has managed to suggest what it is essentially doing; and he has done this at just the point where he abandons objective criteria to make an intuitive leap inside the form. In a Warton Lecture of 1925 which remains the best study of the dramatic monologue, M.W. MacCallum sees sympathy as its way of meaning:

> But in every instance . . . the object [of the dramatic monologue] is to give facts from within. A certain dramatic understanding of the person speaking, which implies a certain dramatic sympathy with him, is not only the essential condition, but the final cause of the whole species.

Unfortunately, MacCallum does not pursue the implications of this insight. If he had, he would not be so disposed to isolate the dramatic monologue within the Victorian period, and he would not confine his consideration to its quality as a monologue. Although the fact that a poem is a monologue helps to determine our sympathy for the speaker, since we must adopt his viewpoint as our entry into the poem, the monologue quality remains nevertheless a means, and not the only means, to the end—the end being to establish the reader's sympathetic relation to the poem, to give him "facts from within."

The distinction may seem niggling unless we see that, by subordinating the dramatic monologue's quality as a monologue to the larger question of the reader's relation to it, we are able to understand the wider connections of the form. For to give facts from within, to derive meaning that is from the poetic material itself rather than from an external standard of judgment, is the specifically romantic contribution to literature; while sympathy or projectiveness, what the Germans call *Einfühlung*, is the specifically romantic way of knowing. Once we consider the dramatic monologue as a poetry of sympathy, we are in a position to see the connection not only between the dramatic monologues of the nineteenth and twentieth centuries but between the dramatic monologue and all that is unprecedented in poetry since the latter eighteenth century. We can see in the differences between the dramatic monologue on the one hand, and the dramatic lyric and lyrical drama of the romanticists on the other, the articulation of a form potential in romantic poetry from the start.

The standard account of the dramatic monologue is that Browning and Tennyson conceived it as a reaction against the romantic confessional style. This is probably true. Both poets had been stung by unfriendly criticism of certain early poems in which they had too much revealed themselves; and both poets published, in 1842, volumes which were a new departure in their careers and which contained dramatic monologues. The personal sting was probably responsible for Tennyson's decade of silence before 1842; it was almost certainly responsible for the disclaimer attached by Browning to his 1842 *Dramatic Lyrics:* "so many utterances of so many imaginary persons, not mine." Yet the reserve of the two poets cannot explain the coincidence that, working independently, they both arrived at the same form and produced at first try dramatic monologues so perfect (Browning's *My Last Duchess* and Tennyson's *Ulysses* and *St Simeon Stylites*) that they were never themselves to surpass them. We must look for precedents; we must suspect that they inherited a form which required only one more step in its development to achieve the objectivity they desired.

Browning's poetry before 1842 suggests by the manner of its failure the kind of precedent that lay behind the dramatic monologue, and the kind of problem that remained for the dramatic monologue to solve. His first published work, *Pauline* (1833), is the poem in which he too much revealed himself. It is transparently autobiographical (although the fictitious identity of the lady addressed provides a disguise of a sort), tracing the poet's intellectual development up to the age of twenty, the time of writing. It was of *Pauline* that John Stuart Mill said: "The writer seems to me possessed with a more intense and morbid self-consciousness than I ever knew in any sane human being"—a criticism Browning took so to heart that he would not allow *Pauline* to be published again until 1867;

and then with an apologetic preface which repeats the disclaimer of 1842: "The thing was my earliest attempt at 'poetry always dramatic in principle, and so many utterances of so many imaginary persons, not mine.' " In spite of which disclaimer, he is reported to have said in his old age that "his early poems were so transparent in their meaning as to draw down upon him the ridicule of the critics, and that, boy as he was, this ridicule and censure stung him into quite another style of writing."

We can follow his attempts at "another style" in *Paracelsus* (1835), a dramatic poem, and *Sordello* (1833–40), an historical narrative. There is, however, little enough drama in *Paracelsus,* and the narrative line is at best intermittent in *Sordello;* in both poems the style that takes over is the introspective, transparently autobiographical history of a soul in the manner of *Pauline*—the soul being in all three recognizable as the same passionately idealistic and endlessly ambitious, endlessly self-absorbed disciple of Shelley. In the preface to the first edition of *Paracelsus,* Browning says that he has reversed the usual method of drama:

> Instead of having recourse to an external machinery of incidents to create and evolve the crisis I desire to produce, I have ventured to display somewhat minutely the mood itself in its rise and progress, and have suffered the agency by which it is influenced and determined to be generally discernible in its effects alone, and subordinate throughout, if not altogether excluded.

And reflecting in 1863 on the failure of *Sordello,* he says in the preface dedicating the new edition of the poem to his friend, the French critic Milsand: "My stress lay on the incidents in the development of a soul: little else is worth study. I, at least, always thought so—you, with many known and unknown to me, think so—others may one day think so."

Did Browning forget that the romantic poets had thought so, that even Arnold, who disagreed, could hardly help but write poetry as though he too thought so, and that the enormous popularity of the "spasmodic" poets gave evidence that by mid-century almost everyone thought so? The question is perhaps answered by Milsand, who, in reviewing *Men and Women* for the *Revue Contemporaine* of September 1856, describes Browning's dramatic monologues in terms applicable to the whole of what I have been calling the poetry of experience. "What Mr Browning has attempted," says Milsand, "is the fusion of two kinds of poetry into one." And after citing Browning's remarks in the *Essay on Shelley* on the distinction between subjective and objective poetry:

> This alone indicates that he sympathizes equally with both kinds of inspiration, and I am inclined to think that from the beginning, and

partly without his knowing it, his constant effort has been to reconcile and combine them, in order to find a way of being, not in turn but simultaneously, lyric and dramatic, subjective and pictorial . . . [His poetry] would have us conceive the inner significance of things by making us see their exteriors.

Compare these remarks of Milsand and Browning with Wordsworth's: "the feeling therein developed gives importance to the action and situation, and not the action and situation to the feeling," and with Pound's description of his own poetry:

To me the short so-called dramatic lyric—at any rate the sort of thing I do—is the poetic part of a drama the rest of which (to me the prose part) is left to the reader's imagination or implied or set in a short note. I catch the character I happen to be interested in at the moment he interests me, usually a moment of song, self-analysis, or sudden under-standing or revelation. And the rest of the play would bore me and presumably the reader.

Add to the comparison Pound's idea that drama is less poetic than other kinds of poetry because "the maximum charge of verbal meaning cannot be used on the stage," and Virginia Woolf's aim "to saturate" in her novels "every atom":

I mean to eliminate all waste, deadness, superfluity: to give the moment whole; whatever it includes. . . . Waste, deadness, come from the inclu-sion of things that don't belong to the moment; this appalling narrative business of the realist: getting on from lunch to dinner: it is false, unreal, merely conventional. Why admit anything to literature that is not poetry—by which I mean saturated?

And we see Browning's innovations as part of a general change of sensibility—a demand that all literature yield much the same effect, an effect of lyrical intensity.

When we have said all the objective things about Browning's *My Last Duchess*, we will not have arrived at the meaning until we point out what can only be substantiated by an appeal to effect—that moral judg-ment does not figure importantly in our response to the duke, that we even identify ourselves with him. But how is such an effect produced in a poem about a cruel Italian duke of the Renaissance who out of unreason-able jealousy has had his last duchess put to death, and is now about to contract a second marriage for the sake of dowry? Certainly, no summary or paraphrase would indicate that condemnation is not our principal response. The difference must be laid to form, to that extra quantity which makes the difference in artistic discourse between content and meaning.

The objective fact that the poem is made up entirely of the duke's utterance has of course much to do with the final meaning, and it is important to say that the poem is in form a monologue. But much more remains to be said about the way in which the content is laid out, before we can come near accounting for the whole meaning. It is important that the duke tells the story of his kind and generous last duchess to, of all people, the envoy from his prospective duchess. It is important that he tells his story while showing off to the envoy the artistic merits of a portrait of the last duchess. It is above all important that the duke carries off his outrageous indiscretion, proceeding triumphantly in the end downstairs to conclude arrangements for the dowry. All this is important not only as content but also as form, because it establishes a relation between the duke on the one hand, and the portrait and the envoy on the other, which determines the reader's relation to the duke and therefore to the poem—which determines, in other words, the poem's meaning.

The utter outrageousness of the duke's behaviour makes condemnation the least interesting response, certainly not the response that can account for the poem's success. What interests us more than the duke's wickedness is his immense attractiveness. His conviction of matchless superiority, his intelligence and bland amorality, his poise, his taste for art, his manners—high-handed aristocratic manners that break the ordinary rules and assert the duke's superiority when he is being most solicitous of the envoy, waiving their difference of rank ("Nay, we'll go/Together down, sir"); these qualities overwhelm the envoy, causing him apparently to suspend judgment of the duke, for he raises no demur. The reader is no less overwhelmed. We suspend moral judgment because we prefer to participate in the duke's power and freedom, in his hard core of character fiercely loyal to itself. Moral judgment is in fact important as the thing to be suspended, as a measure of the price we pay for the privilege of appreciating to the full this extraordinary man.

It is because the duke determines the arrangement and relative subordination of the parts that the poem means what it does. The duchess's goodness shines through the duke's utterance; he makes no attempt to conceal it, so preoccupied is he with his own standard of judgment and so oblivious of the world's. Thus the duchess's case is subordinated to the duke's, the novelty and complexity of which engages our attention. We are busy trying to understand the man who can combine the connoisseur's pride in the lady's beauty with a pride that caused him to murder the lady rather than tell her in what way she displeased him, for in that

> would be some stooping; and I choose
> Never to stoop.

The duke's paradoxical nature is fully revealed when, having boasted how at his command the duchess's life was extinguished, he turns back to the portrait to admire of all things its life-likeness:

> There she stands
> As if alive.

This occurs ten lines from the end, and we might suppose we have by now taken the duke's measure. But the next ten lines produce a series of shocks that outstrip each time our understanding of the duke, and keep us panting after revelation with no opportunity to consolidate our impression of him for moral judgment. For it is at this point that we learn to whom he has been talking; and he goes on to talk about dowry, even allowing himself to murmur the hypocritical assurance that the new bride's self and not the dowry is of course his object. It seems to me that one side of the duke's nature is here stretched as far as it will go; the dazzling figure threatens to decline into paltriness admitting moral judgment, when Browning retrieves it with two brilliant strokes. First, there is the lordly waiving of rank's privilege as the duke and the envoy are about to proceed downstairs, and then there is the perfect all-revealing gesture of the last two and a half lines when the duke stops to show off yet another object in his collection:

> Notice Neptune, though,
> Taming a sea-horse, thought a rarity,
> Which Claus of Innsbruck cast in bronze for me!

The lines bring all the parts of the poem into final combination, with just the relative values that constitute the poem's meaning. The nobleman does not hurry on his way to business, the connoisseur cannot resist showing off yet another precious object, the possessive egotist counts up his possessions even as he moves toward the acquirement of a new possession, a well-dowered bride; and most important, the last duchess is seen in final perspective. She takes her place as one of a line of objects in an art collection; her sad story becomes the *cicerone's* anecdote lending piquancy to the portrait. The duke has taken from her what he wants, her beauty, and thrown the life away; and we watch with awe as he proceeds to take what he wants from the envoy and by implication from the new duchess. He carries all before him by sheer force of will so undeflected by ordinary compunctions as even, I think, to call into question—the question rushes into place behind the startling illumination of the last lines, and lingers as the poem's haunting afternote—the duke's sanity.

The duke reveals all this about himself, grows to his full stature, because we allow him to have his way with us; we subordinate all other considerations to the business of understanding him. If we allowed indignation, or pity for the duchess, to take over when the duke moves from his account of the murder to admire the life-likeness of the portrait, the poem could hold no further surprises for us; it could not even go on to reinforce our judgment as to the duke's wickedness, since the duke does not grow in wickedness after the account of the murder. He grows in strength of character, and in the arrogance and poise which enable him to continue command of the situation after his confession of murder has threatened to turn it against him. To take the full measure of the duke's distinction we must be less concerned to condemn than to appreciate the triumphant transition by which he ignores clean out of existence any judgment of his story that the envoy might have presumed to invent. We must be concerned to appreciate the exquisite timing of the duke's delay over Neptune, to appreciate its fidelity to the duke's own inner rhythm as he tries once more the envoy's already sorely tried patience, and as he teases the reader too by delaying for a lordly whim the poem's conclusion. This willingness of the reader to understand the duke, even to sympathize with him as a necessary condition of reading the poem, is the key to the poem's form. It alone is responsible for a meaning not inherent in the content itself but determined peculiarly by the treatment.

I have chosen My Last Duchess to illustrate the working of sympathy, just because the duke's egregious villainy makes especially apparent the split between moral judgment and our actual feeling for him. The poem carries to the limit an effect peculiarly the genius of the dramatic monologue—I mean the effect created by the tension between sympathy and moral judgment. Although we seldom meet again such an unmitigated villain as the duke, it is safe to say that most successful dramatic monologues deal with speakers who are in some way reprehensible.

Browning delighted in making a case for the apparently immoral position; and the dramatic monologue, since it requires sympathy for the speaker as a condition of reading the poem, is an excellent vehicle for the "impossible" case. Mr. Sludge and Bishop Blougram in matters of the spirit, Prince Hohenstiel—Schwangau in politics, and in love Don Juan of Fifine, are all Machiavellians who defend themselves by an amoral casuistry. The combination of villain and aesthete creates an especially strong tension, and Browning exploits the combination not only in My Last Duchess but again in The Bishop Orders His Tomb, where the dying

Renaissance bishop reveals his venality and shocking perversion of Christianity together with his undeniable taste for magnificence:

> Some lump, ah God, of *lapis lazuli*,
> Big as a Jew's head cut off at the nape,
> Blue as a vein o'er the Madonna's breast

and again in *The Laboratory*, where the Rococo court lady is much concerned with the colour of the poison she buys and would like

> To carry pure death in an earring, a casket,
> A signet, a fan-mount, a filigree basket!

To the extent that these poems are successful, we admire the speaker for his power of intellect (as in *Blougram*) or for his aesthetic passion and sheer passion for living (as in *The Bishop Orders His Tomb*). Hohenstiel-Schwangau and *Fifine* are not successful because no outline of character emerges from the intricacy of the argument, there is no one to sympathize with and we are therefore not convinced even though the arguments are every bit as good as in the successful poems. Arguments cannot make the case in the dramatic monologue but only passion, power, strength of will and intellect, just those existential virtues which are independent of logical and moral correctness and are therefore best made out through sympathy and when clearly separated from, even opposed to, the other virtues. Browning's contemporaries accused him of "perversity" because they found it necessary to sympathize with his reprehensible characters.

But Browning's perversity is intellectual and moral in the sense that most of his characters have taken up their extraordinary positions through a perfectly normal act of will. Tennyson, on the other hand, although less interested in novel moral positions, goes much farther than Browning in dealing in his successful dramatic monologues with an emotional perversity that verges on the pathological. Morally, Tennyson's *St Simeon Stylites* is a conventional liberal Protestant attack upon asceticism. But the poem is unusual because the saint's passion for a heavenly crown is shown as essentially demonic; his hallucinations, self-loathing and insatiable lust for self-punishment suggest a psyche as diseased (we should nowadays call it sado-masochistic) as the ulcerous flesh he boasts of. St Simeon conceives himself in both body and soul as one disgusting sore:

> Altho' I be the basest of mankind,
> From scalp to sole one slough and crust of sin,

and there is in his advice to his disciples a certain obscene zest:

> Mortify
> Your flesh, like me, with scourges and with thorns;
> Smite, shrink not, spare not.

Browning would have complicated the case against asceticism, he might have emphasized the moral ambiguity presented by the saintly ambition which does not differ in quality from the ambition for money or empire; or if he did simplify, it would be to present the case against ascetic ritualism satirically as in *The Spanish Cloister*. Tennyson, however, is more interested in the psychological ambiguity, pursuing the saint's passion to its obscurely sexual recesses.

Treating a similar example of religious buccaneering, Browning has written in *Johannes Agricola in Meditation* a dramatic monologue of sheer lyric exultation. Johannes is, like St Simeon, on a rampage for salvation and confident of attaining it. But compare with St Simeon's the beauty of Johannes' conception of his own spiritual position:

> There's heaven above, and night by night
> I look right through its gorgeous roof;
> No suns and moons though e'er so bright
> Avail to stop me; splendour-proof
> I keep the broods of stars aloof:
> For I intend to get to God,
> For 'tis to God I speed so fast,
> For in God's breast, my own abode,
> Those shoals of dazzling glory passed,
> I lay my spirit down at last.

Although Browning clearly intends us to disapprove of Johannes' Antinomianism, he complicates the issue by showing the lofty passion that can proceed from the immoral doctrine. Nevertheless, the passion is rationally accounted for by the doctrine; Johannes is a fanatic, one who has gone to a philosophical extreme. A moral and philosophical term like *fanatic* will not suffice, however, to characterize St Simeon; we need also a term out of abnormal psychology. It is interesting to note in this connection that *Johannes Agricola* originally appeared together with *Porphyria's Lover* under the common heading of *Madhouse Cells*, but the poems were later separated and the heading abandoned. Without the heading, there is nothing in *Johannes Agricola* to make us suppose that the speaker is mad, that he is anything more than fanatically devoted to his Antinomian principles. That is because Browning does not, like Tennyson in *St Simeon*, pursue the passion downward to those subrational depths where lurk unsuspected motives.

In *Porphyria's Lover*, the speaker is undoubtedly mad. He strangles

Porphyria with her own hair, as a culminating expression of his love and in order to preserve unchanged the perfect moment of her surrender to him. But even here, Browning is relying upon an extraordinary complication of what still remains a rationally understandable motive. The motive and action are no more unreasonable than in A *Forgiveness*, where we do not consider the speaker or his wife mad. She is unfaithful because of her great love for him, and he eventually forgives her by awarding her hate instead of contempt; she allows the life blood to flow out of her to help his hate pass away in vengeance. The motives in both poems are likely to demonstrate for us rather more ingenuity than madness; and it is generally true that extraordinary motives in Browning come not from disordered subconscious urges but, as in Henry James, from the highest moral and intellectual refinement. . . .

Since the past is understood in the same way that we understand the speaker of the dramatic monologue, the dramatic monologue is an excellent instrument for projecting an historical point of view. For the modern sense of the past involves, on the one hand, a sympathy for the past, a willingness to understand it in its own terms as different from the present; and on the other hand it involves a critical awareness of our own modernity. In the same way, we understand the speaker of the dramatic monologue by sympathizing with him, and yet by remaining aware of the moral judgment we have suspended for the sake of understanding. The combination of sympathy and judgment makes the dramatic monologue suitable for expressing all kinds of extraordinary points of view, whether moral, emotional or historical—since sympathy frees us for the widest possible range of experience, while the critical reservation keeps us aware of how far we are departing. The extraordinary point of view is characteristic of all the best dramatic monologues, the pursuit of experience in all its remotest extensions being the genius of the form.

We are dealing, in other words, with empiricism in literature. The pursuit of all experience corresponds to the scientific pursuit of all knowledge; while the sympathy that is a condition of the dramatic monologue corresponds to the scientific attitude of mind, the willingness to understand everything for its own sake and without consideration of practical or moral value. We might even say that the dramatic monologue takes toward its material the literary equivalent of the scientific attitude—the equivalent being, where men and women are the subject of investigation, the historicizing and psychologizing of judgment.

Certainly the Italian Renaissance setting of My *Last Duchess* helps us to suspend moral judgment of the duke, since we partly at least take an historical view; we accept the combination of villainy with taste and manners as a phenomenon of the Renaissance and of the old aristocratic order generally. The extraordinary combination pleases us the way it would the historian, since it impresses upon us the difference of the past from the present. We cannot, however, entirely historicize our moral judgment in this poem, because the duke's crime is too egregious to support historical generalization. More important, therefore, for the suspension of moral judgment is our psychologizing attitude—our willingness to take up the duke's view of events purely for the sake of understanding him, the more outrageous his view the more illuminating for us the psychological revelation.

In *The Bishop Orders His Tomb*, however, our judgment is mainly historicized, because the bishop's sins are not extraordinary but the universally human venalities couched, significantly for the historian, in the predilections of the Italian Renaissance. Thus, the bishop gives vent to materialism and snobbery by planning a bigger and better tomb than his clerical rival's. This poem can be read as a portrait of the age, our moral judgment of the bishop depending upon our moral judgment of the age. Ruskin praised the poem for its historical validity: "It is nearly all that I said of the Central Renaissance in thirty pages of *The Stones of Venice* put into as many lines"; but being no friend of the Renaissance, this is the spirit of the age he conceived Browning to have caught: "it's worldliness, inconsistency, pride, hypocrisy, ignorance of itself, love of art, of luxury, and of good Latin." Browning, who admired the Renaissance, would have admitted all this but he would have insisted, too, upon the enterprise and robust aliveness of the age. What matters, however, is that Browning has presented an historical image the validity of which we can all agree upon, even if our moral judgments differ as they do about the past itself.

In the same way, our understanding of the duke in *My Last Duchess* has a primary validity which is not disturbed by our differing moral judgments after we have finished reading the poem—it being characteristically the style of the dramatic monologue to present its material empirically, as a fact existing before and apart from moral judgment which remains always secondary and problematical. Even where the speaker is specifically concerned with a moral question, he arrives at his answer empirically, as a necessary outcome of conditions within the poem and not through appeal to an outside moral code. Since these conditions are always psychological and sometimes historical as well—since the answer is determined, in other words, by the speaker's nature and the time he inhabits—the moral meaning is of limited application but enjoys within the limiting conditions of the poem a validity which no subsequent differences in judgment can disturb.

Take as an example Browning's dramatic monologues in defence
of Christianity. Although the poet has undoubtedly an axe to grind, he
maintains a distinction between the undeniable fact of the speaker's
response to the conditions of the poem and the general Christian formulation which the reader may or may not draw for himself. The speaker starts
with a blank slate as regards Christianity, and is brought by the conditions
of the poem to a perception of need for the kind of answer provided by
Christianity. Nevertheless, the perception is not expressed in the vocabulary of Christian dogma and the speaker does not himself arrive at a
Christian formulation.

The speakers of the two epistolary monologues, *Karshish* and *Cleon*,
are first-century pagans brought by the historical moment and their own
psychological requirements to perceive the need for a God of Love
(*Karshish*) and a promise of personal immortality (*Cleon*). But they arrive
at the perception through secular concepts, and are prevented by these
same concepts from embracing the Christian answer that lies before them.
Karshish is an Arab physician travelling in Judea who reports the case of
the risen Lazarus as a medical curiosity, regarding Jesus as some master
physician with the cure for a disease that simulates death. He is ashamed,
writing to his medical teacher, of the story's mystical suggestions and
purposely mixes it up with, and even tries to subordinate it to, reports of
cures and medicinal herbs. Yet it is clear throughout that the story haunts
him, and he has already apologized for taking up so much space with it
when he interrupts himself in a magnificent final outburst that reveals the
story's impact upon his deepest feelings:

> The very God! Think, Abib; dost thou think?
> So, the All-Great, were the All-Loving too—.

Nevertheless, he returns in the last line to the scientific judgment,
calling Lazarus a madman and using to characterize the story the same
words he has used to characterize other medical curiosities: "it is strange."

Cleon is a Greek of the last period; master of poetry, painting,
sculpture, music, philosophy, he sums up within himself the whole Greek
cultural accomplishment. Yet writing to a Greek Tyrant who possesses all
that Greek material culture can afford, he encourages the Tyrant's despair
by describing his own. The fruits of culture—self-consciousness and the
increased capacity for joy—are curses, he says, since they only heighten
our awareness that we must die without ever having tasted the joy our
refinement has taught us to conceive. He demonstrates conclusively, in
the manner of the Greek dialectic, that life without hope of immortality is
unbearable. "It is so horrible," he says,

> I dare at times imagine to my need
> Some future state revealed to us by Zeus,
> Unlimited in capability
> For joy, as this is in desire for joy,
> —To seek which, the joy-hunger forces us.

He despairs because Zeus has not revealed this. Nevertheless, he dismisses in a hasty postscript the pretensions of "one called Paulus," "a mere barbarian Jew," to have "access to a secret shut from us."

The need for Christianity stands as empiric fact in these poems, just because it appears in spite of intellectual and cultural objections. In *Saul* there are no objections, but the need is still empiric in that it appears before the Christian formulation of it. The young David sings to Saul of God's love, of His sacrifice for man, and His gift of eternal life, because he needs to sing of the highest conceivable joy, his songs about lesser joys having failed to dispel Saul's depression. David "induces" God's love for Saul from his own, God's willingness to suffer for Saul from his own willingness, and God's gift of eternal life from his own desire to offer Saul the most precious gift possible.

> O Saul,
> it shall be
> A Face like my face that receives thee; a Man
> like to me,
> Thou shalt love and be loved by, for ever:
> a Hand like this hand
> Shall throw open the gates of new life to thee!
> See the Christ stand!

The speaker of A *Death in the Desert* is a Christian—St. John, the beloved disciple and author of the Fourth Gospel, conceived as speaking his last words before dying at a very old age. He has outlived the generation that witnessed the miracles of Christ and the apostles, and has lived to see a generation that questions the promise of Christ's coming and even His existence. As the last living eye-witness, John has been able to reassure this generation; but dying, he leaves a kind of Fifth Gospel for the skeptical generations to follow, generations that will question the existence of John himself. It is an empiricist gospel. "I say, to test man, the proofs shift," says John. But this is well, since belief in God would have no moral effect were it as inevitable as belief in the facts of nature. Myth, man's apprehension of truth, changes; but Truth remains for each generation to rediscover for itself. The later generations will have sufficiently profited from the moral effect of Christianity, so as not to require proof by miracle or direct revelation. They will be able to "induce" God's love from their own and from their need to conceive a love higher than theirs. Thus, Browning invests with dogmatic authority his own anti-dogmatic line of Christian apologetics.

In *Bishop Blougram's Apology*, the case is complicated by the inappropriateness of the speaker and his argument to the Christian principles being defended. Blougram, we are told in an epilogue, "said true things, but called them by wrong names." A Roman Catholic bishop, he has achieved by way of the Church the good things of this world and he points to his success as a sign that he has made the right choice. For his relatively unsuccessful opponent, the agnostic literary man, Gigadibs, the bishop is guilty of hypocrisy, a vice Gigadibs cannot be accused of since he has made no commitments. Since the bishop admits to religious doubt (Gigadibs lives "a life of doubt diversified by faith," the bishop "one of faith diversified by doubt"), Gigadibs can even take pride in a superior respect for religion, he for one not having compromised with belief. Thus, we have the paradox of the compromising worldly Christian against the uncompromising unwordly infidel—a conception demonstrating again Browning's idea that the proofs do not much matter, that there are many proofs better and worse for the same Truth. For if Blougram is right with the wrong reasons, Gigadibs with admirable reasons or at least sentiments is quite wrong.

The point of the poem is that Blougram makes his case, even if on inappropriate grounds. He knows his argument is not the best ("he believed," according to the epilogue, "say, half he spoke"), for the grounds are his opponent's; it is Blougram's achievement that he makes Gigadibs see what the agnostic's proper grounds are. He is doing what Browning does in all the dramatic monologues on religion—making the empiricist argument, starting without any assumptions as to faith and transcendental values. Granting that belief and unbelief are equally problematical, Blougram proceeds to show that even in terms of this world only belief bears fruit while unbelief does not. This is indicated by Blougram's material success, but also by the fact that his moral behaviour, however imperfect, is at least in the direction of his professed principles; whereas Gigadibs' equally moral behaviour is inconsistent with his principles. Who, then, is the hypocrite? "I live my life here," says Blougram; "yours you dare not live."

But the fact remains—and this is the dramatic ambiguity matching the intellectual—that the bishop is no better than his argument, though he can conceive a better argument and a better kind of person. He cannot convert Gigadibs because his argument, for all its suggestion of a Truth higher than itself, must be understood dramatically as rationalizing a selfish world existence. What Gigadibs apparently does learn is that he is no better than the bishop, that he has been the same kind of person after the same kind of rewards only not succeeding so well, and that he has been as intellectually and morally dishonest with his sentimental liberalism as the bishop with his casuistry. All this is suggested indirectly by the last few lines of the epilogue, where we are told that Gigadibs has gone off as a settler to Australia. Rid of false intellectual baggage (the bishop's as well as his own), he will presumably start again from the beginning, "inducing" the Truth for himself. "I hope," says Browning,

> By this time he has tested his first plough,
> And studied his last chapter of St John.

St John, note, who makes the empiricist argument in A Death in the Desert, and whose Gospel Browning admired because of its philosophical rather than thaumaturgic treatment of Christianity.

Although Blougram and A Death in the Desert are too discursive to communicate their religious perceptions in the manner of Karshish, Cleon and Saul, as the speaker's immediate experience, they make their case empirically because they speak in non-Christian terms. They might be considered as setting forth the rhetorical method of the more dramatic poems, a method for being taken seriously as intelligent and modern when broaching religion to the skeptical post-Enlightenment mind. The reader is assumed to be Gigadibs (it is because the bishop is so intelligent that Gigadibs finds it difficult to understand how he can believe), and the poet makes for his benefit a kind of "minimum argument," taking off from his grounds and obtruding no dogmatic assertions.

Eliot addresses his religious poetry to the same kind of reader, communicating his religious perceptions in terms that fall short of Christian dogma. This is especially interesting in Eliot since his concern has been with dogmatic religion, whereas Browning was always anti-dogmatic. Of course, the method is in both poets not merely a deliberate rhetorical device but the necessary outcome of their own religious uncertainties, and a sign that they share like Blougram the post-Enlightenment mind. This is again especially apparent in Eliot, who has dramatized in his poetry his movement from skepticism to orthodoxy, whereas Browning's poetry shows no significant religious development. Nevertheless, there is something of the obtuseness of Karshish and Cleon in those speakers of Eliot's dramatic monologues whose religious perceptions fall short of the Christian truth— and with the same effect as in Browning, that the reader can give assent to the speaker's experience without having to agree on doctrine.

In Journey of the Magi, one of the Magi describes with great clarity and detail the hardships of the journey to Bethlehem, but cannot say for certain what he saw there or what it meant. The Magi returned to their Kingdoms, like Karshish and Cleon "no longer at ease here, in the old dispensation," but still without light. The old Jew Simeon, in *A Song for Simeon*, is somewhat in the position of Browning's David in *Saul*; he sees clearly the glory of Christianity, but is too old to embrace it— not for him "the ultimate vision," the new dispensation is ahead of his time. In *Marina*, the speaker apparently finds the ultimate vision in the face of his newly recovered daughter and in the woodthrush song through the fog, but the vision is still not intelligible, not translated into Christian terms.

In the earlier skeptical poems, the fog is even thicker and no song of revelation comes through it. But Eliot uses idolatrous or "minimum" analogues to the Christian myth to indicate the groping for meaning, his own groping and that of the characters within the poem. The characters in *Gerontion* and *The Waste Land* practise idolatries, aesthetic and occult-ist. *Gerontion* ends with an occultist vision of the modern, cosmopolitan, unbelieving dead whirled around the universe on a meaningless wind:

> De Bailhache, Fresca, Mrs Cammel, whirled
> Beyond the circuit of the shuddering Bear
> In fractured atoms.

Yet seen in the subsequent lines as a natural phenomenon, the wind has a certain meaning in that it unites the parts of nature, north and south, into a single living whole:

> Gull against the wind, in the windy straits
> Of Belle Isle, or running on the Horn,
> White feathers in the snow, the Gulf claims,

and there is, I think, the suggestion that the wind may be a cleansing wind, one which may bring the rain the aged speaker has been waiting for. The same wind that carries off the dead may bring renewal to the depleted living; that is as much meaning and as much hope as the speaker can achieve.

It is as much meaning as our pagan ancestors achieved in the primitive vegetation myths of death and renewal, and Eliot uses the analogy of these myths to give at least that much meaning to the jumbled fragments of *The Waste Land*. Just as the vegetation gods were slain so they might rise renewed and restore the fertility of the land; so the longing for death, which pervades the modern waste land, is a longing for renewal and, if the reader wants to carry the analogy a step farther, a longing for redemption through the blood of Christ, the slain God.

The analogy with the vegetation myths is maintained even in the *Four Quartets*, which are written from a solidly orthodox position. The religious perceptions of these poems are couched less in Christian terms than in terms of that mystical fusion of anthropology and psychology, of myth and the unconscious, that Jung effected. One wonders if the *Four Quartets* are not, for all their orthodoxy, more satisfying to the skeptical than to the orthodox, since the latter might well prefer an articulation of religious truth no less explicit than their own convictions. Post-Enlightenment minds, on the other hand, are particularly fascinated by the mystique of myth and the unconscious as a way back, I think, to a kind of religious speculation which commits them to nothing while preserving intact their status as intelligent, scientific and modern. Myth and the unconscious are contemporary equivalents of Browning's pragmatism in making the "minimum" argument for Christianity.

Although not the only way to talk religion empirically, the dramatic monologue offers certain advantages to the poet who is not committed to a religious position, or who is addressing readers not committed and not wanting to be. The use of the speaker enables him to dramatize a position the possibilities of which he may want to explore as Browning explores the "impossible" case. The speaker also enables him to dramatize an emotional apprehension in advance of or in conflict with his intellectual convictions—a disequilibrium perhaps inevitable to that mind which I have been calling post-Enlightenment or romantic because, having been intellectually through the Enlightenment, it tries to re-establish some spiritual possibility. Browning's St. John, in *A Death in the Desert*, defends religious myths as the expression of just this disequilibrium, of the emotional apprehension that exceeds formulated knowledge:

> man knows partly but conceives beside,
> Creeps ever on from fancies to the fact,
> And in this striving, this converting air
> Into a solid he may grasp and use,
> Finds progress, man's distinctive mark alone,
> Not God's, and not the beasts'.

Even Eliot who professes to be against this "dissociation" of emotional apprehension from its formulated articulation (which for him is dogma), even in Eliot's poetry emotion is always a step ahead of reason—as for example the dim adumbrations of Christianity provided by the vegetation mythology of *The Waste Land*, or the disturbance of the Magi that exceeds their understanding, or that ultimate vision in *Marina*, the articulation of which is obscured by the fog.

Not only can the speaker of the dramatic monologue dramatize a position to which the poet is not ready to commit himself intellectually, but the sympathy which we give the speaker for the sake of the poem and apart from judgment makes it possible for the reader to participate in a position, to see what it feels like to believe that way, without having finally to agree. There is, in other words, the same split between sympathy and judgment that we saw at work in our relation to the duke of *My Last Duchess.* The split is naturally the poem and apart from judgment makes it possible for the reader to participate in a position, to see what it feels like to believe that way, without having finally to agree. There is, in other words, the same split between sympathy and judgment that we saw at work in those dramatic monologues where the speaker is in some way reprehensible, where sympathy is in conflict with judgment, but it is also at work where sympathy is congruent with judgment although a step ahead of it. The split must in fact be at work to some degree, if the poem is to generate the effect which makes it a dramatic monologue.

Browning's *Rabbi Ben Ezra* is a dramatic monologue by virtue of its title only; otherwise it is a direct statement of a philosophical idea, because there is no characterization or setting. Because the statement is not conditioned by a speaker and a situation, there is no way of apprehending it other than intellectually; there is no split between its validity as somebody's apprehension and its objective validity as an idea. But in *Abt Vogler,* where the statement is also approved of, it is conditioned by the speaker's ecstasy as he extemporizes on the organ. His sublime vision of his music as annihilating the distinction between heaven and earth has validity as part of the ecstatic experience of extemporizing, but becomes a matter of philosophical conjecture as the ecstasy subsides and the music modulates back into the "C Major of this life." The disequilibrium between the empiric vision that lasts as long as the ecstasy and the music, and its philosophical implication, makes sympathy operative; and the tension between what is known through sympathy and what is only hypothesized through judgment generates the effect characteristic of the dramatic monologue.

Since sympathy is the primary law of the dramatic monologue, how does judgment get established at all? How does the poet make clear what we are to think of the speaker and his statement? Sometimes it is not clear. The Catholic reader might well consider Tennyson's St Simeon admirable and holy. Readers still try to decide whether Browning is for or against Bishop Blougram. Browning was surprised at accusations of anti-Catholicism that followed the publication of the poem, but he was even more surprised when Cardinal Wiseman (the model for Blougram) wrote in reviewing the poem for a Catholic journal: *"we should never feel surprise at his [Browning's] conversion."* We now know, at least from external evidence if not from more careful reading, that Browning's final judgment is against Don Juan of *Fifine* and Prince Hohenstiel-Schwangau (representing Napoleon III). But the reviewers considered that he was defending the incontinent Don Juan and accused him of perversity; while of *Hohenstiel-Schwangau,* one reviewer said that it was a "eulogism on the Second Empire," and another called it "a scandalous attack on the old constant friend of England."

But these are exceptional cases, occurring mainly in Browning and the result partly of Browning's sometimes excessive ingenuity, partly of a judgment more complex than the reader is expecting, partly of careless reading. Certainly Don Juan's desertion of his wife and return to the gipsy girl in the end—even though he says it is for five minutes and "to clear the matter up"—ought for the careful reader to show up his argument as rationalizing a weak character, although the argument contains in itself much that is valid. In the same way, the final reference to Gigadibs as starting from the beginning with a plough and the Gospel of St John ought to indicate that he is getting closer to the truth than Blougram. I have tried to indicate that more is involved in our judgment of the bishop than the simple alternatives of *for* and *against.* As the bishop himself says of the modern interest in character, which interest is precisely the material of the dramatic monologue:

> Our interest's on the dangerous edge of things.
> The honest thief, the tender murderer,
> The superstitious atheist, demirep
> That loves and saves her soul in new French books—
> We watch while these in equilibrium keep
> The giddy line midway: one step aside,
> They're classed and done with. I, then, keep the line
> Before your sages,—just the men to shrink
> From the gross weights, coarse scales and labels broad
> You offer their refinement. Fool or knave?
> Why needs a bishop be a fool or knave
> When there's a thousand diamond weights between?

There is judgment all right among modern empiricists, but it follows understanding and remains tentative and subordinate to it. In trying to take into account as many facts as possible and to be as supple and complex as the facts themselves, judgment cuts across the conventional categories, often dealing in paradoxes—the honest thief, the tender murderer. Above all, it brings no ready-made yardstick; but allows the case to establish itself in all its particularity, and to be judged according to criteria generated by its particularity.

In other words, judgment is largely psychologized and historicized. We adopt a man's point of view and the point of view of his age in order to judge him—which makes the judgment relative, limited in applicability to the particular conditions of the case. This is the kind of judgment we get in the dramatic monologue, which is for this reason an appropriate form for an empiricist and relativist age, an age which has come to consider value as an evolving thing dependent upon the changing individual and social requirements of the historical process. For such an age judgment can never be final, it has changed and will change again; it must be perpetually checked against fact, which comes before judgment and remains always more certain.

ISOBEL ARMSTRONG

"Mr Sludge, 'The Medium' "

When Mr Sludge, 'The Medium' was
first published in *Dramatis Personae* in 1864, the poem aroused some
controversy. It was a provocative attack on spiritualism, and the portrait
of Sludge was based on a living figure, the American medium, Daniel
Home, who later attempted to defend his reputation. Since this early
controversy and for fairly obvious reasons, *Mr Sludge* has attracted little
attention, and recent critics of Browning's dramatic monologues have not
had much to say about the poem. Because spiritualism is a dead issue, the
subject of the poem seems recondite; the confession and self-justification
of a quack medium suggest merely a study in eccentric psychology and an
exercise in casuistry for its own sake. Even Browning's success in evoking
the mean world of Sludge probably deters readers; the subterfuges of a
trick séance, shoddy credulity and cynical suspicion, sentimentality, hys-
teria, prurience and eager self-titillation ('Let Sludge go on; we'll fancy it's
in print!' [629]) appear gratuitously sordid. But Browning seems to have
seen in the subject an opportunity for writing more than a topical poem,
which would expose spiritualist chicanery, and it is by looking at the way
in which he exploited his dramatic situation—a medium on the defensive—
that this can be understood. The strategy of the medium's defense gave
him a unique way of exploring some arguments about the nature of truth,
knowledge and the imagination, questions which recur in his poetry. In
the course of the poem, these arguments develop startling implications,
and their force depends directly upon the dramatic context in which they
are set. Very little of the detail is gratuitous. In *Mr Sludge* Browning
chose a dramatic situation which would amplify the ideas he explored;

From *Victorian Poetry*, vol.2 (1964). Copyright © 1964 by West Virginia University.

which would, in fact, make it seem inevitable that they should be explored.

It is necessary, in the first place, to understand the importance of Sludge's position as a medium. Even though he has been caught in the act of cheating, Sludge maintains ultimately that he is the authentic agent of spiritual truth, 'seer of the supernatural' (875). There is some 'mode of intercourse/Between us men here' and the spiritual world, he claims (834–5). In effect, Sludge is making the same claims as other of Browning's visionaries. The speaker in *Christmas-Eve and Easter-Day* (1850), for instance, asserts that he has been granted insight into spiritual truth by special revelation. David, in *Saul* (in the final version in *Men and Women*, 1855), discovers that he is the chosen agent, or medium, of God's truth—'Oh speak! through me now!' (299). In *Abt Vogler*, which appeared at the same time as *Mr Sludge* in *Dramatis Personae*, the musician attributes his imaginative vision also to special revelation—'But God has a few of us whom he whispers in the ear' (XI). In the sense that special insight is granted to and interpreted by these visionaries, they are 'mediums'. Sludge, 'inspired', as he says, by the wine of his patron (Hiram E. Horsefall's champagne is a sophisticated variant of the traditional wine of inspiration, analogous with the 'soul-wine' which inspires David in *Saul*), is the degraded equivalent of these visionary prophets. In him the medium shifts from seer to charlatan, and expressions of the truth and authenticity of visionary experience are thus transposed, so as to appear as special pleading from the mouth of a quack. Inevitably they become suspect because the context of sham and shiftiness in which they are expressed undermines them. This sharply exposes the problems which the claim to authentic insight involves—the nature of truth, the limits of knowledge.

Besides presenting the idea of the medium in a pejorative rather than a praiseworthy way in *Mr Sludge*, Browning puts into Sludge's mouth arguments which often parallel those he himself had used apparently seriously, in other poems. Here, with slight shifts of emphasis and modification, they are parodied, and the arguments are used in such a way that they are discredited. At important points in his defense, which turns on the question of truth, Sludge illustrates his case by referring either to the workings of religious belief—a fairly obvious gambit for a spiritualist—or, a less obvious but important move, to the workings of the imagination. Sometimes he makes an analogy with religion or art, most frequently with literature, to support his case (thus contaminating both with the doubtful implications of the practices he tries to justify), and sometimes he uses arguments commonly used to defend the position of the religious believer or the artist, in support of his own position. At these points the arguments (which become suspect if they can be used in Sludge's defense at all) resemble those which Browning had used elsewhere in his poetry. This suggests that Browning may have found in *Mr Sludge* an opportunity for examining critically certain of his own assumptions. In outlining the manoeuvres by which Sludge defends himself, therefore, it will be instructive to concentrate upon those parts of the poem which parody the positions which Browning had taken up on previous occasions.

There are three stages in Sludge's argument. The first stage of his defense occupies roughly the first half of the poem. Rather surprisingly, instead of pleading from the outset that he is a genuine medium, he offers to confess and tell the secret of his deceptions if his patron will agree to release him. In the extensive account of his trickery which follows, he seems to be conceding his guilt to his accuser, but the implicit object of his confession is to destroy confidence in the possibility of discovering truth empirically. His audience had felt certain of his authenticity because they had subjected him to what satisfied them as objective and empirical tests (see, for instance, ll. 488–94), and in this sense they believed in him on rational grounds. But he has deceived his audience with credible 'evidence', and if what seemed conclusively established was actually false, then the certainty of proof is undermined. By invalidating the notion of intellectual certainty, Sludge turns the obvious line of attack to his advantage. Empirical methods have exposed him, but before this they seemed to establish his authenticity, and are therefore unreliable; consequently, if we have no means of discovering whether somebody is telling the truth, we have no means of discovering whether he is lying. Instead of defending himself by an appeal to reason, he satirizes unsparingly those who purported to believe him on rational grounds. Rational men, he says, are 'eunuchs' playing coldly and impotently with superstition. He gives a ludicrous account of the pompous empiricist who dilates spiritualism at dinner parties and proves 'how much common sense he'll hack and hew / I' the critical minute 'twixt the soup and fish' (778–9). The associations of greed and coarseness which the dinner-party situation adds to the common metaphor of logic-chopping suggest the clumsy inadequateness of reason as a means of discovering the truth.

By undermining the notion of intellectual certainty, Sludge prepares the ground for the second part of his defense. When he has put the issue of truth outside the terms of reason, and suggested that the intellect cannot be a means to knowledge, he can safely make an appeal to uncertainty. It cannot be ascertained that he is authentic, but equally, it cannot be ascertained that he is not. Can his audience, can even Sludge himself, be quite sure that he is cheating? Sludge reaches the climax of his argument, justifying his mediumship by the very factors which should undermine it, asking audaciously,

> 'You've found me out in cheating!' That's enough
> To make an apostle swear! Why, when I cheat,
> *Mean to cheat, do cheat, and am caught in the act,*
> *Are you, or, rather, am I sure o' the fact?*
>
> (1281–4)

It may be that his lies are 'genuine' and 'That every cheat's inspired, and every lie / Quick with a germ of truth' (1324–5).

Sludge's position is impregnable, but the implications of his argument are not reassuring. The cost of defending a position by making an appeal to uncertainty is that there are now no criteria for judging 'authenticity'. A philosophical deadlock is inevitable; in denying your adversary the means of proving you wrong, you also deprive yourself of the means of defending your position. What is the nature of the assumptions we make when we say we believe something to be true? Does the operation of belief differ from that of credulity? from superstition? These are the questions raised by Sludge's arguments. The charlatan as well as the seer appears to be invulnerable. Paradoxically, he can only claim that he is in possession of the truth by undermining the validity of the ways in which it might be ascertained. The word 'truth' is always on Sludge's lips, but his arguments deprive it of meaning, and it is constantly devalued. The verbal metaphor here, for instance, condemns his use of the word. 'I can't help that / It's truth! I somehow vomit truth today' (807–8).

This second stage of Sludge's argument marks the point at which he turns from freely confessing to justifying his position. It is in this part of the poem that the references to religion become frequent. 'As for religion—why, I served it, sir!' he asserts.

> With my *phenomena*
> I laid the atheist sprawling on his back,
> Propped up Saint Paul, or, at least, Swedenborg!
>
> (665–7)

Sludge has already insinuated that in the sphere of the spiritual and the supernatural our judgment is fallible and insecure; now, by this explicit reference to religious belief, he shows that he and God are in analogous positions. By transference, all that he has said of his own case is applicable to belief in God. Doubt in his powers, doubt in God (and the verb 'propped up' suggests that God's case is as flimsy as his own), operate in exactly the same way. Conversely, we can accept his authenticity on the same grounds as we accept the existence of God. This enables Sludge to reinforce his appeal to uncertainty by using arguments commonly used to support religious positions. For instance, it may no longer be possible to adhere to a miraculous explanation of the universe, but he still believes in an 'unseen agency' which prompts and directs our actions (a parody of the argument of the first cause), and he himself, tricks and all, might well be the unconscious vehicle of divine purpose. Perversely enough, religious belief supports his position and at the same time the grounds for belief are made to seem ludicrous. Again, he asserts his belief that God is immanent in creation. Just as the merest detail of creation is significant of divine power, so for Sludge, supernatural power is manifest in any trivial occurrence—'the pure *obvious* supernatural'—and he simply interprets the divine immanence more liberally than most.

> What's a star?
> A world, or a world's sun: doesn't it serve
> As taper also, time-piece, weather-glass,
> And almanac? Are stars not set for signs
> When we should shear our sheep, sow corn, prune trees?
> The Bible says so.
>
> (914–19)

This absurdly trivial proposition contrasts ironically with the ecstatic celebration of this idea in *Saul*. David finds the whole universe significant of divine power. 'And the stars of night beat with emotion . . . the strong pain of pent knowledge' (319–20). In Sludge's terms it is impossible to distinguish between the two insights, the medium's or the seer's. It is impossible to 'distinguish between gift and gift, / Washington's oracle and Sludge's itch' (1179–80).

At the end of the poem, Sludge reverses his policy. In the third and last stage of his defense, he admits that he may well have been lying, but if this is the case, he will claim the same kind of 'truth' for his deceptions as that claimed by imaginative writers. His deceptions have performed the same function as the imagination because they have revitalized the lives of his audience—'so, Sludge lies! / Why, he's at worst your poet' (1435–6). He has prepared the way for this discussion of the imagination by making seemingly casual references to the function of art in earlier parts of the poem, and again, because he can invoke art to his support, the function of the artist is called into question. In the first stage of his defense, for instance, while confessing to trickery, he attempts to minimize its importance by comparing his lies to the 'lies' of the artist, and raises directly the problem of the artist's 'truth'.

> Now mark! To be precise—
> Though I say, 'lies' all these, at this first stage,

'Tis just for science' sake: I call such grubs
By the name of what they'll turn to, dragonflies.
Strictly, it's what good people style untruth;
But yet, so far, not quite the full-grown thing:
It's fancying, fable-making, nonsense-work—
What never meant to be so very bad—
The knack of story-telling, brightening up
Each dull old bit of fact that drops its shine.
One does see somewhat when one shuts one's eyes,
If only spots and streaks.

(184–95)

This is an example of contaminating by analogy. Art is trivialized ('nonsense-work', 'story-telling') by being equated with trivial deception. The working of the imagination becomes a matter of slick manipulation, a shoddy knack which merely serves the function of 'brightening up' the world, and 'brightening up' carries with it the pejorative associations of surface-gilding, artificial veneer, synthetic restoration. There is no distinction here between 'fable-making' and deliberate falsification, so that art comes to be regarded as a sophisticated way of lying. The factitious accuracy of the distinction between 'lies' and 'untruths' and the spurious honesty with which Sludge points to the 'genuineness' of imaginative insight ('One does see somewhat when one shuts one's eyes . . .') only serve to enforce the equation of deception with art. Sludge exploits slippery language here, and his ingratiating showman's patter—hustling alliteration, deft, time-saving compounds alternating with sharp syllabic words, the persuasive repetition of synonymous phrases, rhetorical parentheses—hurries over distinctions. But his words counteract one another subtly. Browning allows the language to work in different directions. Lies, for instance, are likened in the first place to grubs, with the suggestion of a pun (insects, dirt), and, when telling a lie is compared a few lines later with the process of 'brightening up', the suggestion of dirt lends a suspect tawdriness to the brightening-up image, destroying the innocuousness which Sludge wishes to claim for his lies.

The connection of the imagination with the false and the trivial dirt, tawdry glitter and flimsy decoration is sustained in other references to art and the artist. These culminate in the discussion of the imagination at the end of the poem, when Sludge abandons all pretensions to the truth. He holds at last that his real function is to renew hope in existence. Like the 'deceptions' of the work of imagination, his deceptions 'reanimate' the lives of those who believe him.

Young, you've force
Wasted like well-streams: old,—oh, then indeed,

> Behold a labyrinth of hydraulic pipes
> Through which you'd play off wondrous waterwork;
> Only, no water's left to feed their play.
>
> (1367–70)

Only he can transform the aridity of life:

> There's your world!
>   Give it me! I slap it brisk
> With harlequin's pasteboard sceptre; what's it now?
> Changed like a rock-flat, rough with rusty weed,
> At first wash-over o' the returning wave!
> All the dry dead impracticable stuff
> Starts into life and light again; this world
> Pervaded by the influx from the next.
> I cheat, and what's the happy consequence?
> You find full justice straightway dealt you out,
> Each want supplied, each ignorance set at ease,
> Each folly fooled.
>
> (1390–1400)

This imagery of machinery, water and conjuring trick closely parallels and parodies three metaphors used in a discussion of the function of the poet in Book Three of *Sordello* (1840). There, temporarily abandoning the method of impersonal narration, which he had followed up to this point, Browning describes the poet as the usurper of God. In syntax which suggests the wrenching effort of performing a superhuman act, he compares the poet to Moses, the bringer of water to the desert, miraculously life-giving and regenerating:

> —each dromedary lolls a tongue,
> Each camel churns a sick and frothy chap
>
> While awkwardly enough your Moses smites
> The rock, though he forego his Promised Land
> Thereby, have Satan claim his carcass, and
> Figure as Metaphysic Poet . . . ah
> Mark ye the first dim oozings?
> (*Sordello*, III, 820–1, 826–30)

He describes a mode of existence which denies the power of the imagination as an arid and mechanistic condition of life, entirely encroached on by the devitalizing forces of rational and scientific thought, and presents an ironic picture of a dead, mechanistic universe, 'pray that I be not busy slitting steel / Or shredding brass . . . before / I name a tithe o' the wheels I trust I do!' [III, 858–61]. Sludge's 'labyrinth of hydraulic pipes' corresponds with this image, but the transforming rod of Moses has become harlequin's gimcrack sceptre.

In perverting these images of regeneration, Sludge adds new force to the ancient charge that the work of imagination is no means to truth and knowledge because it deceives; all that he says of the imagination suggests that it is an insidiously debasing, corrupting agency. He describes the world he offers as a palace of art, enticing its inhabitants with a substitute world of enervating, solipsist fantasy:

> Thus it goes on, not quite like life perhaps,
> But so near, that the very difference piques
>
> And you arrive at the palace: all half real,
> And you, to suit it, less than real beside,
> In a dream, lethargic kind of death in life.
>   (1410–11, 1415–17)

The image recalls the 'palace of music' which is created by Abt Vogler, and which signifies an ideal imaginative world of supreme and perfect order. But Sludge, who also pleads that he provides a 'Golden Age, old Paradise, / Or new Eutopia!' (1431–2), debases the concept of the poet's golden world. He ends his case by identifying the imagination straightforwardly with deception. It is strange, he suggests, that he should be accused of lying, while the writer who boasts, ' 'Tis fancy all; no particle of fact' (1464), merits the highest praise; he is compared with God. As he mimics the praise given to the artist, Sludge mimics the idea of the artist-God which was so important to Browning.

> '—Ah, the more wonderful the gift in you,
> The more creativeness and godlike craft!'
>   (1468–9)

Sludge's patron lets him go instead of exposing him as he had threatened, and perhaps this testifies to the skill of his argument. Certainly, Browning spares nothing in exposing the religious and aesthetic problems arising from the medium's claim to authentic insight and spiritual vision. The poem puts to the test propositions about truth and belief and demonstrates their weaknesses. It challenges a consideration of the status of the untruths of the imagination. Sludge's nihilism may condemn itself, and his methods of persuasion—the alternation of extremes of arrogance with extremes of obsequiousness, calculated showmanship, inadvertent self-pity—may discredit him, but the problems he poses are genuine. In particular, there is the problem of the integrity of the creative imagination. Sludge, simultaneously quack and 'artist', has an affinity with a group of characters through whom Browning explored the theme of the artist whose powers carry with them an inherent possibility of corruption—the poets of *Pauline* (1833) and *Sordello* (1840), Aristophanes in *Aristophanes' Apology* (1875), for instance—and he demonstrates the problem in an acute form. Of course, in poems written both before and after *Mr Sludge,* Browning affirmed an optimistic belief in transcendental insight and the power of the imagination (*Christmas-Eve and Easter-Day* [1850], *Saul* [1855], *Abt Vogler* [1864]), but it would be difficult to see optimism in *Mr Sludge,* let alone the simple-minded optimism with which Browning is sometimes associated.

GEORGE M. RIDENOUR

Four Modes in the Poetry of Robert Browning

I will tell
My state as though 'twere none of mine.

—BROWNING, *Pauline,* lines 585-86

I build on contrasts to discover, above those contrasts, the
harmony of the whole.

—HUGO VON HOFMANNSTHAL
to Richard Strauss, June 15, 1911

Browning was always fiercely Protestant, even when he was not especially Christian. He grew up largely by himself, finding companions in his family, in pets, and in the great number of books he read from his father's large library. His contacts with school were brief and not very satisfactory, and his formal education came largely from private tutors and, perhaps, his father. A try at university life, in the newly established University of London, was soon abandoned, and Browning continued to live with his parents, supported by his father, until his marriage in 1846.

The circumstances of his bringing up were certainly instrumental in developing that "clear consciousness / Of self, distinct from all its qualities" that the young man—with perplexity, pride, and dismay—recognized as central to his character. His problem was what to make of so energetic an ego.

In his poem *Pauline* (published 1833), where he first defined the problem as he understood it, Browning goes on to consider two further "elements" of his character that served as checks on his consuming selfhood. The first is his power of imagination and the second his yearning after God. His imagination is an "angel" to him that sustains "a soul with such desire / Confined to clay." ("Clay" is an obsessive word with Byron, and its use here reminds us that Browning's early poems—destroyed by their author—were supposed to be in the manner of Byron, whom Browning is recalling, along with Shelley, in *Pauline*. There is strong influence of Byron's "Dream.") It enables him to master his "dark past." But the imagination itself poses problems of direction and control which are solved by the premise of a divine Love which presents itself to him as goal and as surrounding presence. The forces united for the boy in the myths of ancient Greece, which enabled his ego to exercise itself healthfully in imaginings of godlike life, and these early experiences of integration remain to some extent normative for him. It is experience of this sort he wants to regain as he addresses himself in *Pauline* to more radical representatives of imagination and religion—Shelley and Christ. It is this he seeks also from the woman Pauline, with her all-encompassing love, who is also the muse of the poem. (It was something very like this that he found in his love for his wife, a woman of deep piety and a poet.)

A similar view is presented sequentially in the speech of the dying Paracelsus, in Browning's drama of that name, defining a progression from the most primitive form of being to man, and from man to God. Two traditions have been traced by scholars here. There is that of man as the culmination of all lower forms, moving steadily toward God, and taking the whole creation with him into the divine life, which Browning might have been more likely to know in an occult version, though it is found in orthodoxy. And there is the more narrowly eighteenth-century tradition of plenitude and the chain of being that may, I suggest, have some obligation to James Thomson, author of *The Seasons*.

> By swift degrees the love of nature works,
> And warms the bosom; till at last, sublimed
> To rapture and enthusiastic heat,
> We feel the present Deity, and take
> The joy of God to see a happy world.
>
> (*Spring*, lines 899–903)

> God is ever present, ever felt,
> In the void waste as in the city full,
> And where he vital spreads there must be joy.
> ("Hymn to the Seasons," lines 105–7)

The two traditions unite in *Paracelsus* V, 641–47, where the hero claims to have known

> what God is, what we are,
> What life is—how God tastes an infinite joy
> In infinite ways—one everlasting bliss,
> From whom all being emanates, all power
> Proceeds; in whom is life for evermore,
> Yet whom existence in its lowest form
> Includes; where dwells enjoyment there is he.

Browning's combination of the two traditions presents a view that is in effect anticipatory of Teilhard de Chardin's vision of an unbroken progression from the geological to the biological to the mental, and on to the divine, each stage once manifest revealing its implicit presence in all preceding stages.

The vision of Paracelsus does not in itself, however, provide means for its implementation in other kinds of poems. It was only after years of attempts at writing a successful play for the stage that Browning fully developed the form of the dramatic monologue, brought to its maturity in the two volumes of *Men and Women* of 1855. Through this succession of self-preoccupied egoists, engaged in existential defense of the being each has made for himself, Browning, as J. Hillis Miller has pointed out, is able both to exercise his own ego and "get out of himself" by objectifying his drive to egoistic self-assertion in the creation of fictional characters. When we have noticed that in the course of their self-revelation they further reveal in their personal situation, directly or indirectly, the intensely Protestant version of the Incarnation that was Browning's governing myth, we can see how the monologues meet the demands of the earlier poems.

Browning's speakers in the monologues are apt to be persons of extremes in extreme situations. Even so winning a character as Lippo Lippi has something grotesque about him and displays an element of the pathologically self-dramatizing, in excess of what might be ascribed to the demands of the form. But like Dostoyevsky or the early Wordsworth, Browning uses his strange or abnormal types to dramatize what he regards as centrally human, which can be seen in these cases with especial clarity. In the following lines, for example, in which Fra Lippo lists the subjects of his first attempts as painter, he reveals not only his own personal situation but that of all men as Browning sees it:

> First, every sort of monk, the black and white,
> I drew them, fat and lean; then, folk at church,
> From good old gossips waiting to confess
> Their cribs of barrel-droppings, candle-ends—
> To the breathless fellow at the altar-foot,
> Fresh from his murder, safe and sitting there
> With the little children round him in a row
> Of admiration, half for his beard and half
> For that white anger of his victim's son
> Shaking a fist at him with one fierce arm,
> Signing himself with the other because of Christ
> (Whose sad face on the cross sees only this
> After the passion of a thousand years)
> Till some poor girl, her apron o'er her head,
> (Which the intense eyes looked through) came at eve
> On tiptoe, said a word, dropped in a loaf,
> Her pair of earrings and a bunch of flowers
> (The brute took growling), prayed, and so was gone.
>
> (lines 145–62)

Here he elaborates the pictorial qualities implicit in the scene of the breathless murderer, the admiring children, the frustrated vindictiveness of the victim's son, and the girl's thankless devotion to the criminal—passions that arrange themselves by their inherent forces of attraction and repulsion into a satisfying composition. The picture is "placed" against another genre, that of the Man of Sorrows on the Cross. It is the world of the painting that Lippo is presented as gaining for art, but he himself sees it as under the judgment of the second, more traditional and more static mode. The exhibition of non-moral human energies, however fine, asks the complement of the image of the dying God. The assimilation of the world of the painting into art has the effect of censuring it as life, but also, since the censor gains much of his authority by his presence to us in art, of encouraging us to enjoy the beauty produced by intense experience of any kind.

It must be confessed, however, that our main impression from the passage is less one of harmony than of competing claims that are hard to choose between, and the feeling grows that Browning's aim as a poet in the Romantic tradition is to devise forms in which the elements of reality as he experiences it may be contemplated as unified. (There seems to be at least a shift in emphasis in the development of Browning's poetry from problems of internal integration to those of perceiving reality itself as an integrated whole.) The list of attempted unions is imposing: power and love, love and knowledge, knowledge and power, imagination and reason, self and not-self, conscious and unconscious, spirit and matter, natural and supernatural, lyric and discursive, verse and prose. His attempts may usefully be broken down into at least four major types: the personal, the typical, the mythic, and the analytic. We may take "Fra Lippo Lippi" as representing the first, the vision of the dramatic monologues, where divisions are overcome in living, or which point toward harmony ironically through the dissonances of the speaker's life. The typical, mythic, and analytic modes, while not inherently more valuable, are in some ways harder to grasp, and it may be helpful to pay special attention to them. The modes will be examined by means of comment on poems drawn, like "Fra Lippo Lippi," from the great work of Browning's middle period, the *Men and Women* of 1855.

What I have called the typical mode may be seen most clearly in "Childe Roland to the Dark Tower Came." It is this typicality that causes our uneasiness in either calling the poem an allegory or in refraining from doing so. The knightly quest lends itself easily to allegorical treatment, because we are all of us looking for something all the time, in all our acts. The formality of the poem also encourages us to think of it as allegorical, even though it is not clear at once what it is allegorical of. This is especially striking since the allegorical mode invites simple and mechanical equation between the contents of the work and the world of values outside it. (This is true of even so refined a work as *The Faerie Queene*, as in the head-verses to the separate cantos. Though the poem is not limited to these crude equations, they influence our understanding of the dense and irreducible materials of the poem proper.) The allegory of "Childe Roland," in other words, is strangely self-contained, turning back on itself, so that the "allegoricalness" of the poem calls attention to itself as part of the meaning.

To shift the terms, allegory is apt to be strikingly rational and subrational, presenting a moral and conceptual organizing of the materials of fantasy; the moral will enters into close union with fierce unconscious drives. In Browning's poem the relations between the two elements are uncommonly problematic. This also tends to turn our attention into the poem in a manner unexpected in allegory, while we are still expecting the poem to fulfil its implied promise to be allegorical of something. One might be tempted to say, then, that the poem is an allegory of allegorizing (with Hawthorne's *Scarlet Letter* as partial analogy). But this would be too narrow, since the allegorical element is a metaphor of our attempts at directing our acts and at understanding them as purposive. It serves to represent the element of moral will in our acts and our understanding of those acts as directed by the moral will. It corresponds to our attempts, that is, at acting humanly for human goals—as "knights." The poem understood in this way becomes an allegory of what is involved in apparently purposeful human acts. It is "typical" of them.

Since the *geste* of Browning's knight is largely a trial by landscape, it may be useful to examine the handling of landscape in another poem, published in the same volume but apparently written later. In "Two in the Campagna" a woman speaks of her inability to love completely and constantly the man she addresses. She loves him only so much and for only so long. Her confession is placed against the reaches of the Roman Campagna, on a May morning.

> The champaign with its endless fleece
>   Of feathery grasses everywhere!
> Silence and passion, joy and peace,
>   An everlasting wash of air—
> Rome's ghost since her decease.
>
> Such life here, through such lengths of hours,
>   Such miracles performed in play,
> Such primal naked forms of flowers,
>   Such letting nature have her way
> While heaven looks from its towers.
>
> (lines 21–30)

The setting suggests, through its vast extent, vast ranges of possibility, and the impression is reinforced by the burgeoning life of early spring. At the same time, however, it suggests immedicable solitude and a tendency in the nature of things for life to squander itself, dispersedly, to no effect:

>   Must I go
> Still like the thistle-ball, no bar,
>   Onward, whenever light winds blow,
>   Fixed by no friendly star?
>
> (lines 52–55)

Man's state and nature's correspond in their interplay of possibility and restriction, freedom and slavery: "Nor yours nor mine, nor slave nor free!" But the emphasis is on defeat.

These passages should recall the landscape of "Childe Roland":

> For mark! no sooner was I fairly found
>   Pledged to the plain, after a pace or two,
>   Than, pausing to throw backward a last view

> O'er the safe road, 'twas gone; gray plain all round;
> Nothing but plain to the horizon's bound.
> I might go on; naught else remained to do.
>
> (lines 49–54)

Here the extent of plain works similarly, with important differences. The possibilities are as great, the limitations more oppressive, and we get a feeling of stuffiness in a wide expanse. This reflects the mingled purposefulness and purposelessness, will and compulsion in the mind of the knight. But the effect is different from that of the landscape in "Two in the Campagna." The vast and monotonous spaces, as well as their painful contents, diminish, to be sure, the single human being who acts in them, but also "enlarge" him, extend his range, ennoble him. The impression is rather that of Burke's "sublime," with its vision of infinite possibility rising from experience of pain and monotony. "Childe Roland" would seem, then, to celebrate the value of man's acts as he blunders doggedly toward goals which are both commonplace and unique:

> The round squat turret, blind as the fool's heart,
> Built of brown stone, without a counterpart
> In the whole world.
>
> (lines 182–84)

The mythic mode is in some ways similar to what I have called the typical, but the differences are important enough to make distinction worthwhile. The main difference is that the mythic mode attaches its action not merely to a central and recurring form of human experience, but to such a form as shaped and celebrated by the imagination of the race. A version of this is found in "The Heretic's Tragedy," which is presented as "a glimpse from the burning of Jacques du Bourg-Molay, at Paris, A.D. 1314; as distorted by the refraction from Flemish brain to brain, during the course of a couple of centuries." Jacques du Bourg-Molay had been grand master of the Order of the Knights Templar and was burned at the stake for reasons apparently more secular than religious. But he had been formally convicted of crimes against the faith, and was burned as a heretic.

The first thing to be noticed is Browning's emphasis on the fact that the event dealt with in the poem has been *distorted* as the account of it has been passed down orally over a long period of time. It has been distorted by the un-Christian hatred of the pious Christians who cherished the tradition and handed it on, constantly sharpening in their account the hateful elements in it. By the time represented by the composition of the poem, the impiety of the victim has been made so grotesque as to be incredible. We respect Jacques du Bourg-Molay because he is hated so violently by persons of so little moral perception.

But the effect of this malice is not merely to discredit the speakers and to honor the victim. The distortion is also clarifying. The corrosive hatred of the generations of faithful has burned away the accidents of the situation, leaving only an archetype which condemns them still more radically. What one sees in the situation of the master of the Temple, as simplified by hate, suggests typically the state of charity, burning in the flames of love (cf. John of the Cross's *Burning Flame of Love),* and mythically the suffering Master on the cross, exalted by the hatred of his execution-ers. The imagination will tell the truth, it seems, whatever the intent of the imaginer, even as the imaginations of Lippo Lippi, Childe Roland, and the singers of "The Heretic's Tragedy" reveal not merely themselves but permanent forms of truth as the imagination knows them.

The analytic mode, as its name suggests, breaks down experience into its separate elements and examines possibilities of interrelationship. All of the poems so far examined have done this to some extent, but there are poems that set about doing just this. The classical analytic work, in this sense, would be Cervantes' *Don Quixote,* read from a perspectivist viewpoint (i.e., as acting out relationships between the opposed but complementary world views expressed in the figures of Don Quixote and Sancho Panza). Closer to Browning in some ways would be Euripides, his favorite Greek dramatist, who gives many examples of "scenes where a situation is realized first in its lyric, then in its iambic aspect—that is to say, first emotionally, then in its reasoned form." There is a good example in the *Alcestis,* which Browning himself translated, in which Alcestis, dying, celebrates her death and its meaning in song, and then argues it out argumentatively. Euripides "has simply juxtaposed these two aspects of Alcestis' parting from life, rather than leave either incomplete." And though Browning, as A.M. Dale points out, tries to ground the argument psychologically in his rendering of the scene, the comparison is still useful.

There is a still closer resemblance, however, to works by the modern German poet and dramatist Hugo von Hofmannsthal, especially in texts for operas by Richard Strauss. This is especially striking in *Ariadne auf Naxos,* in which the oppositions of kinds of love and views of life—generally, tragic (in Ariadne) and comic (in Zerbinetta)—are united both ironically (as Hofmannsthal partly understood) and actually (as he appar-ently did not grasp) through qualities inherent in all love, and through the "harmony" of Strauss's score. The two points of view expose their weaknesses and strengths, their kinds of opposition and union, within the reconciling medium of music.

It is this last, the use of music to define oppositions which are at the same time harmonized, that reminds one most vividly of Browning, whose poems on music attempt something very similar. If you are worried, as Browning often was, about the relation between fact and value, mind and heart, reason and imagination—summed up generally as an opposition between fact and fancy—music can be very helpful. A musical statement can be more abstract than anything in language and still more sensuous than language can ever be. This may give it a unique closeness to reality and at the same time a quality of remoteness, spirituality, fancifulness. Furthermore, it helps us see the two terms as interchangeable: the abstract pole may suggest both reason and unreality, the sensuous both concrete fact and imaginative sentiment. In more formal terms, either pole may suggest comedy or tragedy, poetry or prose.

Browning's finest achievement in this mode is probably "A Toccata of Galuppi's." Among the oppositions to be worked with here is that between eighteenth-century Italy and nineteenth-century England, as well as that between the "scientist" who speaks and the composer who answers. But it is the scientist who is inclined to put stress on value and the composer whose view is cold and analytic, chilling to the inhabitant of a century that is more humane and less elegant. The scientist's union of fancy and fact is unstable, and Galuppi has denied fancy in the name of fact, though his analysis is carried on in a mode that is itself an expression of fancy—i.e., through art. The main agent of union is the composer's clavichord piece, which both includes and is included by the speech of the scientist.

Within the culture that produced the musical form there are grave differences of caste and point of view, brought out by the relations between Galuppi and his audience. They are aristocrats and he a superior servant; their preoccupation with sexual conquest is the object of his rationalistic contempt. But both rationalism and sensuality are part of the period style, as formalized in its music, and the aristocratic audience is not wholly deceived in enjoying it. Furthermore, they find in Galuppi's art a compassion and solace the composer surely did not intend, but which is built into the formal qualities of the music, since it is in support of human purposes that all art inherently subsists. The music, accordingly, in its expression of the central qualities of its period, is not limited by the points of view of artist or audience. The style at the same time separates and unites within its own period as well as between periods. It is in doing the first that it is able to do the second.

The identification of mode is largely on the basis of relative emphasis. It is useful to notice that a particular poem is engaged in a certain kind of activity with special concentration, but that does not mean that it is not doing other things too. "Fra Lippo Lippi" is primarily an expression of a personal state; both problems and ways of handling them are developed in terms of a vividly realized individual personality. But there are strong elements of other modes. The poem is analytic in its reduction of the problem to a competition between opposed areas of value, typical in that the state is seen as that of all men. In the same way, "Childe Roland" has a strong mythic side, as well as displaying analytic and personal aspects, and "The Heretic's Tragedy" reveals an important typical strain, as was noted in the analysis of the poem. "Galuppi" alone of the poems examined seems to be overwhelmingly in one mode, though even here there are elements of the personal and perhaps the typical.

None of this lessens the value of noticing, however, that all of these strains are united with especial force and clarity in Browning's longest and most ambitious work. *The Ring and the Book* is in this as in other ways the climax of Browning's career. *The Ring and the Book* makes a great point of the claim that it is true, and it is largely in terms of the modes I have defined that this claim is substantiated. (From the point of view of literary history, there are two main traditions of works that claim to be true and build this claim into themselves as part of their meaning. There is the analytic tradition of which *Don Quixote* is exemplary, as we have seen. Works in this tradition often claim to be "true to nature." The other tradition is the mythic, represented by *Paradise Lost*, which claims to be true because the myth it enacts is true. These traditions meet in *The Ring and the Book*.)

In exploring possible relationships between the antitheses it includes, a work in the analytic mode might discover that the opposed elements fit without reduction into mythic form. This is what happens in *The Ring and the Book*, which attempts a sweeping transformation of brutal fact into ideal fancy. In terms of the four modes, *The Ring and the Book* is typical both ironically and unironically. Ironically, it is a typical story of intrigue, adultery, revenge, enacting a recurrent pattern in human affairs. But the irony stems from the fact that it is unironically typical in very different terms, as a type of the action of divine love. Mythically, it reenacts the scandal of a manifestation of the divine in the sordid story of a Jewish wife who bore a child not conceived by her husband, as told by Luke. Analytically, it sees in the unlikely materials of the murder story both a clear opposition between the competing claims of fancy and fact and possibilities of overcoming the division. And both oppositions and possibilities of union are developed in terms of real human beings we are made to care about.

The general outlines of the story are clear enough, and I give it in Browning's own normative account, in the first book, since all of the other accounts given in the course of the poem are to be understood as modulations of this:

> Count Guido Franceschini the Aretine,
> Descended of an ancient house, though poor,
> A beak-nosed bushy-bearded black-haired lord,
> Lean, pallid, low of stature yet robust,
> Fifty years old—having four years ago
> Married Pompilia Comparini, young,
> Good, beautiful, at Rome, where she was born,
> And brought her to Arezzo, where they lived
> Unhappy lives, whatever curse the cause—
> This husband, taking four accomplices,
> Followed his wife to Rome, where she was fled
> From their Arezzo to find peace again,
> In convoy, eight months earlier, of a priest,
> Aretine also, of still nobler birth,
> Giuseppe Caponsacchi—caught her there
> Quiet in a villa on a Christmas night,
> With only Pietro and Violante by,
> Both her putative parents; killed the three,
> Aged, they, seventy each, and she, seventeen
> And, two weeks since, the mother of his babe
> Firstborn and heir to what the style was worth
> O' the Guido who determined, dared and did
> This deed just as he purposed point by point.

In this first account, Browning is careful to label Pompilia explicitly as good and to make it pretty clear that for reasons as yet not understood, she was right in what she did and that Guido was wrong. He points up the pathos of the ages of the victims and of the fact that Pompilia was a mother of two weeks. It is less that he is unsure of the self-validating nature of truth or of his own ability to present it adequately than that he does not trust us to read correctly without help. He is conscious of the experimental nature of his poem, and he is not sure that we will be able to keep our bearings. The story of the murder will be told again and again, from different points of view. Some of these, such as the speeches of the "three halves" of Rome, of the lawyers, and of Guido, are exercises in dramatic irony, in which the speaker betrays himself and his own weaknesses, and in doing so makes clear the sense in which, in his version, the truth is being distorted. This is to help us see what then the truth is. In the case of Caponsacchi and, especially, Pompilia, deductions for personal limitations are minimal. What distortion there is tends to be a reflection of their own goodness. And the Pope, it is clear, is presented as entirely authoritative. It is in his vision, Browning would have it, that the truth revealed in the other accounts is contemplated as such, is defined and judged. For "the joke" is that the perplexed circumstances and multiple accounts do not, as we might expect, lead to relativism and an inability to make clear moral judgments, but to a polarizing of the issues into choices between radical good and radical evil, clearly recognizable as such.

It is in the speech of the Pope that all of the modes defined in this introduction manifest themselves with special clarity: typical in the enactment of the archetype of moral judgment; analytic in the understanding of the relation between unlikely fact and fanciful actuality; mythic in its integration of the life and death of Pompilia into that of Christ; personal in its depiction of a rich human being to whom we respond, and in whose personality, as we experience it, the problems raised by the work are persuasively resolved. And it is finally on the personal level, no doubt, that the poem justifies itself, in the vitality of the human beings whose lives raise the issues and offer ways of dealing with them.

It may also be at this level that it is most vulnerable. There is a cold-blooded ferocity in the handling of Guido, for example, by both Caponsacchi and the Pope that has some of the effect of the hatred of the singers of "The Heretic's Tragedy," without, in this case, the excuse of intentional irony. We are to take it all at the speaker's evaluation, and admire the speaker all the more for it. For many readers this may be hard to do. The tone is that of Browning himself at his most viciously self-righteous. It reflects a failing rather common in Browning, who had great faith in the poetic value of his own sentiments.

This weakness is increasingly evident in the volumes that follow *The Ring and the Book*, which tend to impress one as exercises in perversity or as lazy thinking in casual verse. There is nothing comparable to the rich harmonies attained by works of the middle period. Only rarely, as in "La Saisiaz," is he able to integrate argument into an imagined whole, and his success here is precarious. There are brilliant individual pieces in these later books, such as the stunning "Thamuris Marching," or some lyrics of surprising sharpness, but they must be sought out. This makes the success of his final volume, *Asolando*, all the more remarkable and gratifying. While it does not suggest the mellow old age of a Titian or Verdi—it is too thin for that—it is charming and in its way impressive. Browning takes up again his lifetime's preoccupation with "Fancies and Facts" (the subtitle of the volume), and announces his choice in the Prologue of "The naked very thing." But a world so seen is more magical, and not less, in that it points to a transcendent reality beyond itself (in the last lines of the Prologue) and that as our vision of fact becomes clearer, the more clearly we see it encompass the values of fancy (in "Flute Music," or "Development"). The tone of the book is one of delighted acceptance, the manner engagingly playful. It is a fitting *vivace*-finale to Browning's life's work.

JOHN HOLLANDER

Browning:
The Music of Music

English Romantic poetry is strangely
unconcerned with actual instrumental or vocal music. Musical imagery
occurs frequently in Wordsworth, Coleridge, Keats and Shelley when a
response to the perception of some noise in nature is to be rhetorically or
conceptually heightened. But their imaginative concern is largely with the
music, as it were, of sound. With one notable exception in English
nineteenth-century poetry, the tradition of attention to this concern
persists well into the period of dawning symbolist influence, when the
music of poetry itself would come to triumph in power and universality
over the most abstract of quartets, the most visionary of symphonic
poems, which language began striving to emulate. Browning is that exception. His knowledge and experience of, and his lifelong interest in music
have been widely discussed, and recently there has been Professor Ridenour's
profound and acute study of some of the ways in which Browning ab-
stracted from his experience of music modes for representing experience of
the world in general. Browning's detailed musical images are almost
unique in English poetry, however, and they are all the more remarkable
when read against the poet's Romantic heritage. It is easy to describe
them as emblematic, as generating not only new analogies but new
grounds for analogy with each turn of explication. One is reminded of
some of the more conventional musical conceits in seventeenth-century
poems: the sympathetic vibration of two perfectly tuned strings as a type
of love, for example, or even Alciati's venerable emblem of the stringed

From *Striver's Row* 1 (1974). Copyright © 1974 by John Hollander.

instrument, well-tuned, as political unification. But the ways in which Browning's imaginative use of music depart from his heritage are more elusive.

Sometimes, in fact, English Romantic sound imagery will actually take up a Renaissance musical emblem and naturalize it; this is particularly frequent in Shelley, whose imaginative energies delighted in transforming pastoral images of sound into the heightened underscoring of a more immediately envisioned landscape. Even an unacknowledged historical semantic change can serve as a pivoting point, as with the shift of meaning in "sweet" from the seventeenth-century musical sense of "in perfect tune" (cf. modern "sour note" and see Jessica in *The Merchant of Venice* [V, 1]: "I am never merry when I hear sweet music") to the continuing olfactory one, in these lines from *Epipsychidion:*

> And from her lips, as from a hyacinth full
> Of honey-dew, a liquid murmur drops,
> Killing the sense with passion: sweet as stops
> Of planetary music heard in trance.
>
> (83–86)

Here the two meanings blend the human physical senses and reanimate, along with the psychologizing about the trance, what would otherwise be a seventeenth-century cliché. Or even more obviously, about 60 lines further on, a conceit bordering on the quibbling—"We—are we not formed, as notes of music are, / For one another, though dissimilar" —becomes transformed, in the appositive paraphrase of the following lines, from a homely, almost technical musical trope into an image lying in the mainstream of English Romantic musical expression:

> Such difference without discord, as can make
> Those sweetest sounds, in which all spirits shake
> As trembling leaves in a continuous air?
>
> (144–146)

The figure is that of musical sound blending with the natural noise of leaves moving in the air, the mingled measure of human music and the voice of nature. Whether specifically embodied in the symbol of the Aeolian harp (or even more ubiquitous from the mid-eighteenth century on, in complex and surrogate forms of that symbol), the truest music, in English Romantic tradition, was always the least feigning. Eighteenth-century nature poetry had brought a new poetic recognition to the consciousness of outdoor sound, employing both neoclassical and pastoral images of music to describe what was not music at all, but, acoustically speaking, noise. Rooted in pastoral conventions in which natural noises of wind and water and amplifying echo authenticated the poetical truth of utterance within the *locus amoenus,* the music of natural sound in Wordsworth and Coleridge, and in a renewed way in Keats and Shelley, drowns out the sound of cultural music. German Romantic writing is full of deep musico-literary connections, but in England a combination of the backward state of British music and the prime involvement of Romantic vision with the discovery of consciousness by, and in, the open hall of the rural, contrived to trivialize the concert hall, the drawing-room and the opera house as far as the poetic imagination was concerned.

Browning's earliest musical imagery reflects his English tradition, and Shelley in particular, in unsurprising ways. In *Pauline,* the "sweet task" of reading Shelley himself becomes

> To disentangle, gather sense from song:
> Since, song-inwoven, lurked there sense which seemed
> A key to a new world, the muttering
> Of angels, something yet unguessed by man.
>
> (413–416)

Text and music, braided together like thought and feeling in an image of a secondary harmonizing that goes back to Milton's "At a Solemn Music," here yield up a truth that Wordsworth's American progeny would forever strain to hear in the half-decipherable whisperings of nature. In a more German mood, at the end of *Pauline,* the protagonist invokes the inaccessibility of music's transcendent truth, a truth seen to be so much like the power of an eroticized but unyielding nature:

> kissing me when I
> Look up—like summer wind! Be still to me
> A help to music's mystery which mind fails
> To fathom, its solution no mere clue!
>
> (928–931)

In Part II of *Paracelsus,* that ghost of Alastor, the young poet Aprile, limns his vision of the life of art, transforming the world by the very act of describing it in a sequence of projects moving from the sculptural, to the plastic, to the verbal ("Now poured at once forth in a burning flow, / Now piled up to a grand array of words"). The sequence concludes with a final creative act, like a sigh of completion as a maker breathes upon his perfected but still lifeless shapes:

> This done, to perfect and consummate all,
> Even as a luminous haze links star to star,
> I would supply all chasms with music, breathing

> Mysterious motions of the soul, no way
> To be defined save in strange melodies.
> (II, 475–479)

Here is another of the core musical images of Romantic tradition—
the cave, shell or chasm embodying a spirit of sound. Like the mysterious
eloquence of music in *Pauline*, these lines invoke a background of visionary music in its relation to landscape, a background extending back past
Shelley to Wordsworth and the eighteenth century. This *mystique en plein
air*, heard at a distance, remembered from the past dominating English
poetry, might have remained the conceptual source of later musical imagery in Browning, as, in transformations worked upon Keats' versions of it,
it was for Tennyson. But under the pressure of a number of forces, it
virtually disappeared from Browning's world of images, reappearing only at
the end of his career, in the language of the sentimentalist "He" who
hears flute-music through the trees in one of the poems of *Asolando*. The
forces which banish it are various: the developing interest in the minute
particulars of cultural and historical fact under the rhetorical control of
dramatic monologue, for one; a fascination, mentioned earlier, with an
almost seventeenth-century emblematic mode of thought, for another,
and withal Browning's own love and knowledge of music, and the ways in
which this knowledge shaped his listening ear.

This last is a most elusive matter. There has been a good deal of
dispute about the order and depth of Browning's technical musical skill,
and it has been fashionable to deride it. Baldassare Galuppi, for example,
was a Venetian composer of opera primarily, and there seem to be no
known "toccatas" by him. Almost any cultured reader today knows that,
had said protagonist indeed played "stately at the clavichord," he would
have been inaudible in a room full of even temporarily silenced masquers—a
clavichord's tiny, private, touch-responsive tinkle was almost for the ear
of the performer alone. Abt Vogler's descending chromatic sequences are,
in the words of a prominent and prolific Victorian composer, "the refuge of
the destitute amateur improviser." These crude dismissals are easily answered. In the first place, Browning cannot be judged by fairly sophisticated, twentieth-century musicological standards; after all, his own
contemporaries conventionally mistranslated the last word in the title of
Bach's *Das Wohltempierte Klavier* as "clavichord" (it means, generically,
"keyboard"). Although Browning later claimed to have known actual
Galuppian toccatas from ms. volumes, we may assume that he was in fact
filling in, à la Borges, a historical lacuna, and that the stop consonants of
the Italian polysyllable "toccata" tripped across the tongue with an appropriate gallop. And again, the cavalier attribution of works to early com-

posers was ubiquitous in the nineteenth century (the reader with some pianism of his own may observe that the first of the two popular volumes entitled *Early Keyboard Music,* originally compiled in 1904 and still kept in print by Schirmer, contains what purports to be a *"Fuga"* by Frescobaldi: a moment's inspection will reveal that it is a fine academic pastiche of Bach—composed, in fact, by Clementi!). Similarly, the scraps of music Browning himself undoubtedly composed—for the children to sing in *Strafford,* for example ("suitable for children," as DeVane characterized it, but no more "historically accurate" for the seventeenth century than a similar song at an equivalent moment in Donizetti might have been), or for "the lilt (Oh, not sung!)" to which Pietro of Abano's tale is crooned—are amateurish. But not mindlessly so, for they betoken the kind of intimate acquaintance with the actualities of composition and performance that transform musical listening from a passive condition of being played upon, to a kind of active engagement with the flow of structured sound. Compared with selectively hearing melody, or responding to "a rattling good tune"—that curse of the English musical sensibility, as De Quincey so tellingly observed—that active faculty of energized listening is like following a sophisticated argument or thread of discourse, as opposed to understanding merely the spoken language of an utterance. This faculty Browning not only possessed, but wrote about as if he possessed. A mere technical allusion to musical practice, even a clever conceit based on it, is one thing. A grasp of, for example, the dialectic of vertical and horizontal in analytic or even compositional schemata, is another.

For example, when Milton writes in Book XI of *Paradise Lost* about the music of Jubal—Michael is showing Adam a projected vision of the dangers and possibilities of human culture—he reveals tents

> whence the sound
> Of instruments that made melodious chime
> Was heard, of Harp and Organ; and who mov'd
> Their stops and chords was seen: his volant touch
> Instinct through all proportions high and low
> Fled and pursu'd transverse the resonant fugue.
> (XI, 558–563)

Most simply, this is an expansion of the Biblical text in which Jubal figures as the father "of all such as handle the harp and organ." But the virtuoso in the passage, improvising polyphonic keyboard fantasias, is an actual seventeenth-century musician. "His *volant* touch / Instinct" is, given the now-obsolete sense of "touch" to mean a sounded musical phrase, almost synaesthetic, in applying to his flying fingers and the flights of sound which they elicit. The metaphor then follows music flight in another sense, "through all proportions high and low / Fled and pursu'd transverse the resonant fugue." Not only the flight of printed notes on a stave, but the abstract motion of the horizontal parts, the polyphonic voices, *through* high and low intervals (almost in the way that, we might say, a curve flies *through* higher and lower cartesian coordinates), are being figured here. The final revelation of the syntax is that his "volant touch . . . pursu'd transverse the resonant fugue," and the implied elusiveness of the fugue, the musical form, its structure and indeed its notational shape, is underlined by the semantic movement of the whole passage, through the "volant" to the "fled" and, finally, to the "fugue," both in object and in more than resonant name. Aside from all its other brilliancies, the whole passage is mimetic of the act of hearing music when one knows how it is put together, and can perhaps even envision its notation. Such representations of musical experience are very rare indeed in English poetry, as are, in any language, poets capable of producing them.

Browning has almost no immediate predecessors with sufficiently available musical knowledge to enable them to mythologize listening to music as they could do to the wind in the trees, or, in particular, the experience of seeing through and behind the seen. One exception, how- ever, is Leigh Hunt. As both connoisseur and practicing music critic, one might have expected Hunt to have essayed something on the subject of concert music, and indeed he did: "The Fancy-Concert" (1845), a serio- comic extravaganza, written in the anapestic tetrameters of incipient *vers de societe,* and conjuring up an imaginary perfect concert, embracing the history of music from the late Baroque to Beethoven. Then, too, Hunt left some smaller pieces, including one, in a smarmy German manner on "the Lover of Music to His Pianoforte." Of most interest to the problem of getting sophisticated musical experience into poetry, however, are two blank-verse poems, one, a fragment called "Paganini" first published in 1834, and "A Thought on Music" with the subtitle "suggested by a Private Concert, May 13, 1815."

The first of these starts out in the language of an almost conven- tional European contemporary Paganiniolatry, invoking

> the pale magician of the bow,
> Who brought from Italy the tales, made true,
> Of Grecian lyres; and on his sphery hand,
> Loading the air with dumb expectancy,
> Suspended, ere it fell, a nation's breath.
>
> (3–7)

It then goes on to acknowledge the diabolic tincture in the violin- ist's nature by seeing him as "One that had parted with his soul for pride, / And in the sable secret lived forlorn." Continental romantic tradition made much of the demonic, deracinated figure of the musician, from Diderot on. Even in the English seventeenth century, stories were told of the composer and keyboard virtuoso John Bull that affirmed his cloven hoof. Hunt does all but recite Paganiniana about fiddle-strings made from the gut of a dead mistress; but after a while, the tone changes and becomes a frantic, rather Shelleyan effusion of straining effort to keep descriptive pace with the dazzling range of effects of the master's playing. For about 75 lines, the images proliferate in pursuit of the stream of sound, in a pattern perhaps most directly modelled upon the lyrical treatment of mountain streams and cataracts moving rapidly through landscape (Hunt probably could not have known Crashaw's *Musicks Duell,* some of whose descriptions of lute-playing and bird-song his poem suggests). One may cut in almost at random:

> he would overthrow
> That vision with a shower of notes like hail,
> Or sudden mixtures of all difficult things
> Never yet heard; flashing the sharp tones now,
> In downward leaps like swords; now rising fine
> Into some utmost tip of minute sound,
> From whence he stepped into a higher and higher
> On viewless points, till laugh took leave of him:
> Or he would fly as if from all the world
> To be alone and happy, and you should hear
> His instrument become a tree far off,
> A nest of birds and sunbeams, sparkling both,
> A cottage-bower. . . .
>
> (50–63)

Or, perhaps later on, where the resources of Jacobean dramatic verse are called out in aid of hearing and feeling:

> or some twofold strain
> Moving before him in sweet-going yoke,
> Ride like an Eastern conqueror, round whose state
> Some light Morisco leaps with his guitar;
> And ever and anon o'er these he'd throw
> Jets of small notes like pearl, or like the pelt
> Of lovers' sweetmeats on Italian lutes
> From windows on a feast-day, or the leaps
> Of pebbled water, sprinkled in the sun,
> One chord effecting all. . . .
>
> (72–81)

Toward the end of the piece, in its way, a kind of exercise, some attention is paid to the attending consciousness "when the ear / Felt there was nothing present but himself / And silence," for example—but by and large, the genre of the piece is low-mimetic, a step above the devices used by Southey to render the waters coming down at Lodore, perhaps. Much more interesting is the fragment of Hunt's written nearly twenty years earlier. "A Thought on Music" struggles, against what proves to be the ultimately overwhelming power of conventionalized rhetoric about music, epithets and stock responses, to anatomize the act of informed listening. The first sixteen lines represent the English romantic musical experience in miniature, as the more or less specific (if not, in this instance, technical) observations move outdoors from the concert-room, and substitute for the dramaturgy of structure and style in the musical world, the cadences and closures of easily available myth:

> To sit with downward listening, and crossed knee,
> Half conscious, half unconscious, of the throng
> Of fellow-ears, and hear the well-met skill
> Of fine musicians,—the glib ivory
> Twinkling with numerous prevalence,—the snatch
> Of brief and birdy flute, that leaps apart,—
> Giddy violins, that do whate'er they please,—
> And sobering all with circling manliness,
> The bass, uprolling deep and voluble;—
> Well may the sickliest thought, that keeps its home
> In a sad heart, give gentle way for once,
> And quitting its pain-anchored hold, put forth
> On that sweet sea of many-billowed sound,
> Floating and floating in a dreamy lapse,
> Like a half-sleeper in a summer boat,
> Till heaven seems near, and angels travelling by.
> (1–16)

The second part of the poem moves beyond even this, back into the recesses of German romantic musical theory where the very referential vagueness of music, its lack of quasi-linguistic meaning, is held to make it the most universal and poetic of arts. The following lines openly deny the possibility of just the kind of listening a character in Browning, for example, will express:

> For not the notes alone, or new-found air,
> Or structure of elaborate harmonies,
> With steps that to the waiting treble climb,
> Suffice a true-touched ear.
> (17–20)

—and as the meditation resumes, the language, the cadence, the movement of image and example through the argument, become unabashedly Wordsworthian:

> To that will come
> Out of the very vagueness of the joy
> A shaping and a sense of things beyond us,
> Great things and voices great: nor will it reckon
> Sounds, that so wake up the fond-hearted air,
> To be the unmeaning raptures they are held,
> Or mere suggestions of our human feeling,
> Sorrow, or mirth, or triumph. Infinite things
> There are, both small and great, whose worth were lost
> On us alone,—the flies with lavish plumes,—
> The starry-showering snow,—the tints and shapes
> That hide about the flowers,—gigantic trees,
> That crowd for miles up mountain solitudes
> As on the steps of some great natural temple,
> To view the godlike sun:—nor have the clouds
> Only one face, but on the side of heaven
> Keep ever gorgeous beds of golden light.
>
> Part then alone we hear, as part we see;
> And in this music, lovely things of air
> May find a sympathy of heart or tongue,
> Which shook perhaps the master, when he wrote,
> With what he knew not,—meanings exquisite,—
> Thrillings, that have their answering chords in heaven,—
> Perhaps a language well-tuned hearts shall know
> In that blest air, and thus in pipe and string
> Left by angelic mouths to lure us thither.
>
> (20–45)

The poem has moved from a brief encounter with the attempt to render the experience of aware listening, through the evasions of merely literary writing about musical instruments ("And virgin trebles wed the manly bass"—so Marvell in "Music's Empire," and so the cliché thereafter), out to the dream journey in "a summer boat," and finally to a Wordsworthian recognition of the superior power of mythologized nature in accounts of heightened moments of consciousness. Willy-nilly, the English romantic poet, no matter how profound his immersion in the world of musical art, will succumb to the force of the image of the mingled measure, the dispersion of the sounds of human music, vocal or instrumental, in the moving air of landscape. Even the hint of neoplatonizing myth at the end (it combines an older image of sympathetic resonance with association of a spirit of music with moving air imprisoned in a cavity)—and even the cancelled line in Hunt's manuscript (the text given is the published one of 1875) so reminiscent of German romantic musical theory: "Music's the voice of Heaven without the words"—cannot overpower the larger natural vision.

In this vision in eighteenth- and nineteenth century English poetry, the music of order and of Orphean power, so celebrated in the Renaissance and Baroque, gives way to and attention to the music of sound. Romantic myths of consciousness first introduce us to the music of silence—silence in an acoustical, rather than a rhetorical, sense: the soundless, rather than the tacit. But in Browning's mature poetry we are aware of a musical sensibility of a very different sort. What his monologuists hear is the music of music itself; what concerns him is by no means raw sound, nor even embodied feeling—indeed, he is acutely aware of how reductive so many usual readings of musical significances can be. Rather is he attentive to the full flux of musical experience, the apprehension of meanings not in musical sounds themselves, not in modalities of major and minor, rapid and slow alone, but in the very structures of musical art, understood in their stylistic and historical dimensions.

From an early observation, like one of *Paracelsus* about the wind passing "like a dancing psaltress" over the breast of the earth in springtime (a tamed Coleridgean "mad lutanist" and an Aeolian harp image of a conventional type), he can move eventually to a total avowal of the power and significance of instrumental music. It is important to note the distinction between, on the one hand, an older, emblematic concept of instrumental music, by which an Orphean instrument stood for the emotive and persuasive power of music, poetry and eloquence itself, and, on the other, the elevation of "pure"—that is, instrumental—music to a position of highest importance in Continental romantic aesthetic theory. The common view that textless music, being more general, was therefore more universal even than song, depended upon an association of vagueness of referential meaning with states of feeling; it is almost as if, in the frantic quest for pictorial and musical correspondences that we find in some of the speculations of a Wackenroder, of a Runge, instrumental music is doing the imaginative work of landscape, of uninhabited natural scenery, in representing the continuingly unfolding epic of human awareness. A notion far less common in Continental aesthetic tradition, however, gives to the flow of music in time a meaning much more discursive. "Must pure instrumental music not make of itself a text? and does not a theme in it get as developed, confirmed, varied and contrasted as the object of meditation in a philosophical argument?" asks Friedrich Schlegel in a remark somewhat uncharacteristic of a historical moment which proclaims music's flights above and beyond the discursive.

What is ultimately so remarkable about Browning's use of the act of comprehending music listened to, rather than merely heard, is its ability to operate with both of these opposed views. Along with the dialectic of the spatial and temporal images which harmonic and melodic, vertical and horizontal modes of musical perception tend to project; along with music's ability, as Ridenour has so brilliantly shown, to function for Browning as an emblem in the representation of a theory of fictions; we find the more mature musical imagery in Browning's poetry mediating between the lyrical and the discursive even on a theoretical level. "Ah, Music, wouldst thou help!" murmurs Don Juan in *Fifine at the Fair* (ll. 943–945). "Words struggle with the weight / So feebly of the False, thick element between / Our soul, the True, and Truth!"—but the point of the whole following passage is not that music floats above meanings, but that it can sometimes do the work of signifying more effectively, and it concludes with the strange ascription to music of a usually unacknowl-edged attribute: "And since to weary words recourse must be, / At least permit they rest their burden here and there, / Music-like: cover space!" (ll. 961–963) *"Cover space!"*—not by flying above it, nor by being audible at a distance, but rather by filling room: this is conceptual possibility, not a phonetic nor even an auditory phenomenon. The move-ment of thought, not merely feeling, often seems more like music than like sequences of words. In addition, it is confusing, if not actually ironic, that such a notion would occur only to someone able to grasp, in a concrete and "technical" sense, the nature of purely musical thought—someone who, whether or not he might have erred in reading "sixths diminished" into his fictive Galuppi toccata, certainly understood the syntax of sonata-form, the unfolding logic of variation, the architechtonics of structural harmony to any degree.

It is this sense of music's meaning which gradually comes to inform the musical imagery in Browning's poetry. Even where his toying with a conceit is closest to the Donne and Quarles he admired, even where his interlocutors will turn a comparison which they have already faceted like a jewel over and over, that it may catch the light differently, an interest lying behind that of the capability of emblems will be at work. "Clash forth life's common chord, whence, list how there ascend / Harmonics far and faint, till our perception end,— / Reverberated notes whence we construct the scale / Embracing what we know and feel and are!" proposes Don Juan a bit further on in *Fifine at the Fair* (ll. 968–971). The image he uses anticipates what would become in twentieth-century English the cliché of "overtones" (a word introduced into the language only in the 1860's, in fact, to translate Helmholtz's *Oberton,* "harmonic partial") as a German musical parallel to the French, pictorial term "nuances" of significance. But it is not only that acoustical phenomena—harmonics, combination tones, etc., like echoes—or Doppler-effect dying wails of train whistles in nineteenth- or twentieth-century poetry—are figures for meanings, but that the relational connotations of *musical tones,* rather than acoustical noises, have been affirmed in the vehicle of the metaphor itself. It represents the phenomenology of experience in a powerful way: first, there is the almost crude trope, reworked from the earlier "Abt Vogler," of "life's common chord"—the givens of feelings, the routines of sensation—from which emanate the harmonics, barely heard or recorded only in what Leibniz called music's "unconscious arithmetic," reaching up into physical inaudibility as they simultaneously increase in frequency beyond about 15,000 cycles per second, and drop below the threshold of audible amplitude. And yet, and yet . . . it is the harmonics, not the gross packagings of them we discern as tones or triads, which are the atoms of acoustical and hence of musical experience. And so the rumbling of the ordinary world seems to release the increasingly faint ideas, the overtones of consciousness, out of which it is itself ultimately composed.

Such an image, both forceful and accurate, must also be understood as coming from a special kind of experience of listening to music—from brooding over the act of listening through an understanding of the structural causes of the music's sensuous and emotive effects. It is this aspect of listening which Leigh Hunt was unable or unconcerned to figure forth in the early fragment previously noted. We may observe a moment toward the representation of sophisticated listening in all of Browning's music poems. "A Toccata of Galuppi's," to start with, is all talk over music, although there are several levels of audible or fancied discourse, and which is background, which moving against it—which is underscoring and sounding through holes in the other, music or chatter—is always nicely in question. If it were only a matter of his moral about cultural history, Browning might as well have chosen, say, a masque of Inigo Jones' being performed for its doomed Caroline court. The specific function of the music in the poem is to be mimetic of chatter, as the poem's chatter is, indeed, to sound like rapid passage-work (with the brilliant prosodic conflict producing a *ritardando* at its coda: "Dear, dead women, with such hair, too" is jammed into the otherwise unvarying trochaic rhythm). The listener here is an over-hearer of both music and talk.

In "Master Hugues of Saxe-Gotha" the monologuist is the listening musician, responding to the consequences of his own playing; his meditation starts from the historical donné of the exercise by an old master whose very name rhymes with "fugues." The dramaturgy of fugal entrances, of which any listener would be aware, is heightened for the performer by the visual and kinetic dimensions of notational pattern and actual fingerings. In the poem, they are all at work to strengthen the imaginative difference between the execution and the architecture of formal structure, on the one hand, and the final human function, whatever or wherever it may be, on the other. Again, though, it is clear that throughout "Master Hugues" the organist is anchored to a moment in his own musical culture in which "Counterpoint glares like a Gorgon" (as opposed, say, to the taste of the second third of the twentieth century for polyphonic styles of the past in themselves). The intellectual web is spun out, rises and drapes itself, in an unstated pictorial correspondence, over the tracery and other carved stonework in the church's interior, and whether its veil protects, obscures, obliterates or even creatively mediates, remains the unanswered question about tradition and imagination, dwelling in the air like the overhang of echo.

In "Abt Vogler" the meditative structure grows out of the overhang of echoing in the vault of memory; the poem follows the improvisation in time, and the emblematic readings of harmonic progressions in the famous final stanza lead toward a traditional meditative coda, a descent to the ground of ordinary life from the mind's flights, even as the flights of life alight on the beds of sleep and death. Chromatic descent then pauses for a moment on the last momentary peak of a suspension:

> Give me the keys. I feel for the common chord again,
>> Sliding by semitones till I sink to the minor,—yes,
> And I blunt it into a ninth, and I stand on alien ground,
>> Surveying awhile the heights I rolled from into the deep;
> Which, hark, I have dared and done, for my resting-place is found,
>> The C Major of this life: so, now I will try to sleep.
>
> (XII)

"Dared and done" but without the first "determin'd" from the triad in Smart's "A Song to David" which he is echoing—and now even the gross obviousness is appropriate to the image of the quotidian as C Major, easy, "normal," its signature uncluttered with sharps and flats, the Dorian tonality of march, power, order and health translated into classical diatonic conventions. But in an image when the extempore meditation is at its heights, "such gift be allowed to man, / That out of three sounds he frame, not a fourth sound, but a star," there is greater emblematic subtlety: a fundamental process of musical conceptualization, whereby the harmonic triad becomes not only an aural organism more significant than the sum of the meanings of its parts, but a self-sustaining object of attentive wonder, transcending even the embodying medium which generated it. The leap from tone to star is accomplished in something very like a conceit with a hole in it, and itself occurs at a high point of the poem's imaginative structure, paralleling perhaps a tonal peak in the composer's still-resounding improvisation on that small, private organ "of his own invention."

> Consider it well: each tone of our scale in itself is naught:
> 　It is everywhere in the world—loud, soft, and all is said:
> Give it to me to use! I mix it with two in my thought:
> 　And there!
>
> 　　　　　　　　　　　　　　　　　　　　　(VII)

　　Tones are ordinary particulars: music, like architectural structures, like poetry, builds upward as well as outward from its elements, and only from the tops of such buildings can their strength, and their fragility, be perceived.

　　In his "Parleying with Charles Avison" Browning himself becomes one of his monologuist listeners-to-music, but his discourse is with musicology, rather than with any performed composition. It is a moralization of the ruins of the simplistic ancestors of those structural and harmonic complexities of a later age which themselves have caused the crumbling. The presiding muse of the art here is Clio, not Euterpe or Terpsichore; the historical dialectic of stylistic succession as against a mysterious invariance, of attenuation and complexity, finally devolves upon the history of music. But for Browning, music's history is now and England, and Avison's trivial and silly little march tune becomes important because of its author's connection to Browning through a chain of teachers. The Avison poem is very explicit about how "There is no truer truth obtainable / By Man than comes of music." It is also very insistent upon resurrecting the Dorian ethos for a C Major march than can, like most marches, organize human life around it with a crudely Orphean force that all art envies.

　　But as an involved listener, there is no figure to challenge the Don Juan of *Fifine at the Fair*. He is a musical sophisticate like the others, capable of expressing a continuing wonder at the reductions which occur in moving from "Effect, in Art, to cause," still marvelling how music,

> 　　　　　that burst of pillared cloud by day
> And pillared fire by night, was product, must we say,
> Of modulating just, by enharmonic change,—
> The augmented sixth resolved,—from out the straighter range
> Of D sharp minor—leap of disimprisoned thrall—
> Into thy light and life, D major natural?
>
> 　　　　　　　　　　　　　　　　　　(639–641)

The actual harmonic resolution here—a conventional "Italian sixth," probably, pivoting around an enharmonic rewriting of D sharp/E flat—attests less to a musical sensibility than a feeling for the brightness, the "light and life" of the resolved D major.

But Don Juan's listening ear is most aware, both of what it hears and of itself, in the remarkable long section that weaves in and out of memories of Schumann's *Carnaval* (Op. 9). The monologuist has turned to it at a crucial point in his thoughts, hung somewhere between what Kierkegaard's protagonist of the "Either/Or" calls rotation of field and rotation of crops. If Elvire's firmness makes his circle just, he can roam through many arcs, including, for example, Fifine's; a sensibility that knows its Raphael to be central and unwobbling can let its eyes sip Doré. The Fair through which he is walking leads, by a bit of involuntary memory, to the *Carnaval,* and the technique of musical variation as employed in that romantic potpourri becomes the correlative for the wandering eros. In lines 1515 to 1636 of *Fifine at the Fair* we are introduced to what I think is one of the very few anticipations in nineteenth-century literature of Swann's chasing down of his *petite phrase* through the corridors of sentimental association. The Don rehearses his recent keyboard reading of *Carnaval* not merely for its associations with the Pornic Fair, but as a model of an erotic rhythm of sharpened desire and satiation on the familiar:

> I somehow played the piece, remarked on each old theme
> I' the new dress; saw how food o' the soul, the stuff that's made
> To furnish man with thought and feeling, is purveyed
> Substantially the same from age to age, with change
> Of the outside only for successive feasters.
>
> (1912–1616)

He is thinking of Schumann's generation of moods, of the successive "scenes mignonnes" from the "quatre notes" of the anagrammatic "sphinx" motives, of the very assemblage of the character pieces of the work. But he soon concentrates on the desire's banquet of sense, and on the history of taste as its projected image, tracing it along until

> one day, another age by due
> Rotation, pries, sniffs, smacks, discovers old is new,
> And sauce, our sires pronounced insipid, proves again
> Sole piquant, may resume its titillating reign—
> With music, most of all the arts, since change is there
> The law, and not the lapse: the precious means the rare,
> And not the absolute in all good save surprise.
> So I remarked upon our Schumann's victories

> Over the commonplace, how faded phrase grew fine,
> And palled perfection.
>
> (1645–1654)

And when he turns to *Carnaval* in detail, it is, as he says, to Elvire's favorite portion of it,

>   that movement, you prefer,
> Where dance and shuffle past,—he scolding while she pouts,
> She canting while he calms,—in those eternal bouts
> Of age, the dog—with youth, the cat—by rose-festoon
> Tied teasingly enough—Columbine, Pantaloon:
> She, toe-tips and *staccato,*—*legato,* shakes his poll
> And shambles in pursuit, the senior. *Fi la folle!*
> Lie to him! get his gold and pay its price! begin
> Your trade betimes, nor wait till you've wed Harlequin
> And need, at the week's end, to play the duteous wife,
> And swear you still love slaps and leapings more than life!
> Pretty, I say.
>
> (1658–1669)

The Don is, of course, reading himself and his dancing gypsy girl into Schumann's "*Pantalon et Columbine*" piece, and, as in so many other great moments of self-betrayal by speakers in Browning, he is quite unaware of what he is doing. "And so I somehow-nohow played / The whole o' the pretty piece; and then . . ." he continues; if he means here the whole of *Carnaval* (rather than merely the "*Pantalon et Columbine*"), a startling and poignant memory-lapse underlines the authenticity of his proclaimed self-knowledge in a little epiphany of error. "Whatever weighed / My eyes down, furled the films about my wits?" he asks, and immediately goes on to essay an uneasy answer:

>   suppose,
> The morning-bath,—the sweet monotony of those
> Three keys, flat, flat and flat, never a sharp at all,—
> Or else the brain's fatigue, forced even here to fall
> Into the same old track, and recognize the shift
> From old to new, and back to old again, and,—swift
> Or slow, no matter,—still the certainty of change,
> Conviction we shall find the false, where'er we range,
> In art no less than nature.
>
> (1671–1679)

His memory slips. There is indeed a B major section of the "*Reconnaissance*" piece, enharmonically arrived at through the C-flat in an A-flat minor close, and Don Juan's harping on the "sweet monotony" underlines the unavowed self-revelation earlier on. Whether desiring to eat the cake had, or to have the cake eaten, Browning's Don Juan has something of the same relation to Kierkegaard's, of Mozart's, as the protagonist of *Maude* to Hamlet. And though his reading of Schumann may be both consciously tendentious and unknowingly self-absorbed, it is never reductive, as reverie over familiar music can seldom be. In this again, he is one of Browning's most mature listeners.

In Don Juan's available experience, as throughout his work, Browning was using the world of music in all its aspects—those of stylistic history, simpler acoustic theory, the facts of amateur and professional performance, and so forth—much as he could call up those other realms of art and historical melodrama. Particularly in its historical dimension, the spread of formal music lay before him like landscape; and, much like landscape in the poetry of some of his predecessors, provided not merely examples, but modes of exemplification of creative acts of knowledge— mappings as well as maps of the course of truth through the shadowed visible. By the end of his career, the earlier Romantic treatment of music as a conceptual and semantic instrument for the amplification of nature's susurrus might seem simplistic.

It is all the more interesting, then, to turn to "Flute-Music, With an Accompaniment" from the *Asolando* volume, where the entire poem is set in a typical Romantic outdoor musical environment, and "the bird-like fluting / Through the ash-tops yonder" of the opening lines is in itself like an archaic dance or aria theme picked up for a set of *variations brilliantes.* But the old theme is in itself merely archaistic, a clever pastiche—this is not the true mingled measure as one might hear it in Collins, or Bowles, or Wordsworth or Coleridge, the blending of a singer's or instrumentalist's voice with natural sound, or the filtering of that voice through the objects of landscape. This is not the post-pastoral natural music, unruined because never having been brought indoors; it is, rather, the high, formal musical art with which Browning was concerned throughout his career, now, literally, *asolate*—brought outdoors for recess and free play.

As the poem unrolls, *"He"* hears a neighbor's flute-playing, and hears it sentimentally and, as it were, picturesquely: he is a literary listener, and has an ear only for the Love, Hope, Musing and, finally, Acquiescence which, by turns, emanate from the inner source of sound curtained by the ash-tops. *"She,"* on the other hand, hears the music of music, none the less so because, having heard the amateur flautist practice before, she recognizes one of his five easy pieces—in this case, some etude or other by Jean Louis Tulou (a flautist and maker of flutes—whose trademark, one learns from Grove's *Dictionary,* was a nightingale). *She* is amused at what *He* concludes from what his "ear's auxiliar / —Fancy—found suggestive"; *She* can ask

So, 't was distance altered
    Sharps to flats? The missing
Bar when syncopation faltered
    (You thought—paused for kissing!)
Ash-tops too felonious
    Intercepted? Rather
Say—they well-nigh made euphonious
    Discord, helped to gather
Phrase, by phrase, turn patches
    Into simulated
Unity which botching matches,—
    Scraps reintegrated.
                    (133–144)

This is like the half-serious reductiveness of Aldous Huxley's itself reductive version of D. H. Lawrence, Mark Rampion, purporting to hear only the "horsehair on catgut" in Beethoven's quartet Op. 132, as an ad hoc response to Spandrell's mystical reading of it in *Point Counterpoint*. The dialectic is indeed of "fact and fancy" here, as several critics have pointed out. But it also handles, brilliantly as well as playfully, two contrasted versions of the role of music in an imaginative universe. *She* hears the music that goes on in Browning's poetry; *He* hears music of a more visionary sort, taking up, for example, the older theme of "Notes by distance made more sweet"—

Distance—ash-tops aiding
Reconciled scraps less contrarious,
Brightened stuff fast fading.
                    (170–172)

Nevertheless, he is more aware of the human nuances, of the factuality of his visionary hearing for which there is no word. The separate responses of the two are polarized across a line cut by domestic comedy (and by the assignment of the reductive reading to the woman and the problematic one to the man, in a tradition that goes back at least as far as Chaucer's Chaunteclere and Pertelote). Those responses bifurcate a fiction which, in Browning's own rich sense of music, remains uncloven—a blended involvement with musical actuality and with the Imagination's lust for the discovery of signification in all experience. A Browning monologuist would hear all that *He* hears but *in,* not apart from, what *She* does. Their argument can be abandoned, not resolved, in bed; its resolution could only occur in that highest and most self-aware act of listening to music which becomes, through—not despite—its technical consciousness, an attention to the music of humanity.

ELEANOR COOK

"Love Among the Ruins"

L*ove Among the Ruins,* which opened the 1855 *Men and Women,* has some of the same properties as *Two in the Campagna.* It is a poem that once again places a pair of lovers on bare grassy landscape by the remains of a dead city. But the premises and the problems are much different.

A manuscript draft of *Love Among the Ruins* in the Houghton Library at Harvard entitles the poem 'Sicilian Pastoral,' and certainly the requisite properties for a pastoral scene are present. A shepherd and his feeding flock slowly wend their homeward way in a drowsy peaceful twilight; a tryst with a maiden is anticipated, a fair-haired maiden waiting in a turret. The whole to take place on a pastureland covering the ruins of a prosperous but corrupt city of which the turret is the only visible remain. ('Lean neath stone pine the pastor lies with his crook; young pricket by pricket's sister nibbleth on return viridities; amaid her rocking grasses the herb trinity shams lowliness; skyup is of ever-grey.') It is all a fine set piece, and due contrast may be drawn between the wicked city and the pure country, the sinful dead and the virtuous living, worldly glory and private love. This is what the poem is sometimes reduced to. There is only one problem, and that is the speaker, who does not seem to appreciate the scene as he ought.

The contrast in the title is obvious: love alive among the ruins, the relics of the dead; the fresh and new among the old and enduring; the good (pastoral love is always good) among the remains of the not-so-good, the venial, the ambitious, the dishonest, the corrupt. (The contrast simply of alive and dead was mentioned by Elizabeth Barrett in her *Greek*

From *Browning's Lyrics: An Exploration.* Copyright © 1974 by University of Toronto Press.

Christian Poets: 'Wonderful it is to look back fathoms down the great Past, thousands of years away—where whole generations lie unmade to dust—where the sounding of their trumpets, and the rushing of their scythed chariots . . . are more silent than the dog breathing at our feet, or the fly's paces on our window-pane.') No specific indication is given of precisely what ruins Browning has in mind; it would seem that the ruins are a type, and a composite of the remains of several ancient cities.

The speaker begins with his pastureland, moving through it in a slow, meandering rhythm to match the ambling sheep-pace and gradually to stretch out and relax the mind as the land itself stretches out 'where the quiet-coloured end of evening smiles / Miles and miles . . .' Browning uses an internal rhyme in only one other short line, and there too the word is repeated ('ere we extinguish sight and speech / Each on each'—a thud of colliding bodies). Here the effect is to draw our eye out and along the extent of the pastureland, the easier done because it is (except for the lovers) uninhabited. It is sleepy pastoral landscape, with sheep half-asleep as they wander, and it seems to be receiving an evening benison from the setting sun, which smiles on the scene. The rhythm picks up with the city. It is something of a fairy-tale city ('so they say'), which was 'great and gay'; however peaceful the first three lines are, they cannot be described as gay, and that the pasture is undistinguished by marks of greatness, or of anything at all for that matter, the speaker will make clear. The city was the capital, the centre of things, drawing them together; councils came into the city, authority went out from it. Now the site is all circumference and no centre, diffused and dissipated. Except for the streams, the hills would slide into one land-mass, like the indistinguishable waves of the sea, rolling and bare. The city used to stretch into the sky, and in the second stanza the contrast is not between centre and circle but horizontal and vertical. 'Domed and daring,' spires like fires: then even the buildings seemed as alive as flame, unlike the most unfiery present scene where the only fire is the quiet-coloured dying sun. The present is all too earthy and somewhat watery; it is the past that shoots into the air like fire.

In the third stanza the shepherd attempts some unpastoral sarcasm: 'And such plenty and perfection, see, of grass / Never was! / Such a carpet . . .' The romantic city is exerting its spell. Now the shepherd sees himself walking on a carpet of grass which is not springing lush from solid earth, but which embeds the lost city over which he travels. Underneath the verdure the city lies all the while, with its fire now dead, and with all its gold again returned underground. The fluid rolling hills have also become hollow. But in the second half of this stanza, the city, hitherto a fairy-tale type, shifts to a wicked urban type. Glory and shame (a familiar pairing in Browning) were the motives, 'and that glory and that shame alike, the gold / Bought and sold.' Nevertheless the city continues to shed influence. If it is a Sodom or a Babylon, it is a glittering one.

Only a turret now shows the spot where once a tower stood, and it too has fallen prey to greenery, to parasitic vines that mark time and disuse. It is 'over-rooted . . . overscored,' overcome altogether, this remnant of a building that once sprang as the spires shot. Fiery as those spires was the burning ring traced about the tower by racing chariots watched by king, minions, and dames. This present earth melts away altogether in the vision. The quiet colours become undistinguished grey as light vanishes and the hills slip into anonymity. The sun still smiles but now it 'smiles *to* leave' the flock 'in *such* peace', its smile now no evening benison, but an enigmatic, silent leave-taking.

Then comes a new factor: a girl with some of the vitality of the old city in her eager eyes and some of the city's golden allure in her yellow hair. The current monarch, she looks out where the king looked—but no, the figure is wrong, for she does not command, but awaits her lover in order to come alive. Like some princess captive in a tower and under a spell, she is 'breathless, dumb / Till I come.' And in the speaker's mind, even after evoking his beloved's image, the imaginary city still exercises its magic, spreading out building after building—'—and then, / All the men!'" What follows does not lend itself to ready comparison, as in the other stanzas; the two halves seem somewhat unconnected. The king looked far and wide; the lovers will look only at each other (or rather, what the lover says exactly is that she will look only at him), and they will then rush together and extinguish both sight and speech, 'each on each.' To the king, his dominions; to the lovers, their own enclosed and willingly circumscribed kingdom. But again, a disturbing element has been introduced ('—and then, / All the men!'). There is somehow awkwardness in thinking of those men who 'breathed joy and woe/ Long ago.' Then there was the multitude, full of its passion and its goal; now there is one pair.

In the last stanza, the city jumps out of control. It sends out a million fighters; it shoots a pillar to the sky; it retains a thousand golden chariots. It also takes over all the stanza except the last line, for the second half is the somewhat puzzling disposal of the vision:

> O heart! oh blood that freezes, blood that burns!
> Earth's returns
> For whole centuries of folly, noise and sin!
> Shut them in,
> With their triumphs and their glories and the rest!
> Love is best.

Suddenly the earth takes over after all the fire and all the unearthly spurts of growth: the city is returned to its safe underground tomb, with triumphs, glories, *and the rest.*

Love is best, then, better than the gold and glories of the past. In *Night and Morning,* that enigmatic little pair of lyrics, somewhat similar imagery is used, but no indication is given there of who the lovers are or what their situation, or even what the conclusion is. In *Fifine at the Fair,* like imagery of land, village, house represents domestic virtues and the sea the romantic call of adventure, the usage there being very complex. Here the path of gold is the burning ring of the gold chariots or the brazen pillars' spurt toward the sky. The city's movement is swift, aggressive, shooting, and daring. But it has all been domesticated now: the king's tower is a lovers' meeting-place; shepherd and flock merely saunter; the city's gold is reflected only in the girl's muted yellow hair; the magic city has been converted into a cellar above which sheep may safely graze.

It has been shut in with considerable vehemence, however, and the fact that it must be shut in and pushed down, active ghost that it is, shows how alive it has become for the speaker. Why does it grow out of all proportion in the last stanza, and why is the speaker so agitated? Is it a yearning for the path of gold that produces his irony and his disgust with the undistinguished grey and perfection of the grass? If so, why does he not sell the flock and march off to the big city with his golden girl? Perhaps there is some compulsion to stay, but this is never hinted and takes us wildly astray. What is more than hinted is the intense agitation over the idea of the city and its inhabitants.

Here is the place to come back to the shepherd's stereotypes, both of city and men. For the speaker does tend to think in stereotypes and some of them tend to break down. The pastoral archetype turns ironic and mysterious. The city is in the first stanza a casual contrast like an idle thought stumbled on as the shepherd goes to his beloved. By the last stanza the sound is fortissimo, the city has grown up through the ground to the sky and out to the horizon, the vehemence approaches anguish. Curious things happen to the men too: they breathe joy and woe; then what explains them is lust of glory and dread of shame, either one for sale; then their lives are reduced to folly, noise, and sin. If the description of the city is exaggerated, may not that of the men also be? Even the shepherd's lady is conceived in rather stereotyped terms: 'a girl with eager eyes and yellow hair.' Such emphatic contrived contrast suits very well the young shepherd's pattern of thinking. His sarcasms on the plenitude of grass are heavy; his final dismissal, though no solution, is loudly assertive. He seems unlikely to spend a day sitting on the campagna musing on spider-threads. Nor do we hear much about his anticipated good minute. Indeed the attitude of a swain who says coolly that his lady is 'breathless, dumb / Till I come' is interesting. The love among the ruins seems not to have mitigated the anguish, but merely to have suppressed it.

The lover does not pay much attention to his lady though he is on his way to a meeting. Perhaps I am being perverse: he is thinking of something else. But oddly enough the closer he comes to his beloved, the greater his vehemence grows, as if the city posed a direct personal threat to the lovers. When they meet they will extinguish sight and speech, and this includes the mental sight of the city, which so torments the young swain. Shut in by an embrace, he will be able to shut out the city. The noise as he approaches the turret is like the din surrounding Childe Roland as he comes close to the dark tower. Abruptly, with the last three lines, it is cut.

The city has proved altogether too lively for the simple tags assigned to it. There is more to those men than those motives will account for. Once they were as alive as the shepherd now is, and as joyful as he will be when he meets the girl with yellow hair. For the moment he stands apart and he sees one pair alive in the turret above a multitude dead under the carpet of grass. The grass that has grown over all the city's fire and gold will some day grow over the lovers' own vitality. His agitation grows, I think, from the same passion that animates the *Lament for Bion*: 'Alas, when the mallows and green parsley and curly-tendrilled anise perish in the garden, they live once more and grow up another year; but we men . . ."

Grass or plant, especially when it grows over the artifacts and monuments of man, the latter usually stone, is a frequent symbol in Browning of the passage of time and the persistence of the natural cycle. In *Red Cotton Night-Cap Country*, sub-titled *Turf and Towers*, turf represents changeable things, the finite; and rock and tower, what seems durable. When vegetation covers ruins, 'little life begins where great life ends' (1046). In *The Inn Album*, as in *Love Among the Ruins*, grass may prove different from what it first appears: '. . . the grass which grows so thick, he thinks, / Only to pillow him is product just / Of what lies festering beneath!' (2284–6). In *Clive* a crumbling castle may be climbed by any tourist:

> Towers—the heap he kicks now! turrets—just the measure of his cane!
> . . . Observe moreover—(same similitude again)—
> Such a castle seldom crumbles by sheer stress of cannonade:
> 'T is when foes are foiled and fighting's finished that vile rains invade,
> Grass o'ergrows, o'ergrows till night-birds congregating find no holes

Fit to build in like the topmost sockets made for banner-poles.
So Clive crumbled slow in London, crashed at last.

(53–9)

In *Fifine at the Fair*, section lxxxix, there is a tower overgrown by a creeper-branch: the poem's imagery is complex, but notable among the creeper's characteristics is its consciousness of purpose (a flirtatious Fifine purpose, the creeper being invested with incredible sexuality).

The tower itself is a fairly frequent image in Browning, its use being varied and complex. Here it is enough to observe that besides obvious connotations this turret is a remnant of the vertical aspiring city so unlike the flat passive grass. (Cf. these two patterns in *Two in the Campagna*, the latter there being the one that is discarded; the question here is how much the shepherd's love has in common with the flat passive landscape with which he associates it.) The tower is also a place of observation. Elizabeth Barrett more than once uses it in this sense: 'To make a promise is one thing, & to keep it is quite another: & the conclusion you see "as from a tower" ' (*LRBEB*, I, 291; Nov. 24, 1845). 'M. Milsand will not [approve of *Aurora Leigh*], I prophesy; "seeing as from a tower the end of all" ' (*LEB*, II, 242; Nov., 1856. In *Aurora Leigh* 'towers of observation' (849) are for sight. So too is the tower in *Fifine at the Fair*, the sight being of ambiguous value. So too is the tower at the end of *Red Cotton Night-Cap Country*, the sight proving fatal for Miranda. In *Love Among the Ruins* the king surveyed his domains from the tower; perhaps it is important that lover and beloved 'extinguish sight and speech' (and do so 'each on each)' in the turret that remains.

I do not want to press the Bion theme unduly hard. It seems to me unmistakably present, but under the surface of the shepherd's thinking. The lyric that centres on the Bion theme, and it is a not infrequent theme in Browning, is *A Toccata of Galuppi's*. Here what we are left with is simply what the title says: love among the ruins, that is, a contrast. The contrast turns into a conflict as the speaker muses; the conflict becomes an impasse; in a way not immediately apparent to him, this threatens his love; he is impelled to deal forcibly if not persuasively with it; he does so by suppressing one contending half. It is not, after all, surprising that the shepherd does not concentrate on his lady as he approaches her: the poem is about a threat to her and the kind of relation is clearly not one in which she could be of use in meeting the threat. A girl who waits, breathless and dumb, to be awakened by her lover may please his vanity, but is little help in meeting danger with him. That this remark is not irrelevant is, I think, shown by the role Leonor plays in *By the Fireside*. (Browning had a great distaste for passive women: cf. *A Woman's Last Word*, even the woman of

Two in the Campagna, the girl here; he managed to describe their malleable devotion as 'a kind of love' in *Red Cotton Night-Cap Country*, but it is ranked far below the love of a Leonor or a Lyric Love, and his active women are made far more attractive than his passive ones.) The girl with yellow hair will be as protected by her shepherd as she is now sheltered in her turret; left as peaceful as the dumb sheep he also protects, and shepherds to their fold. The city grows wildly in the last stanza because the speaker knows something must be done with it. Either he or his yellow-haired girl makes it impossible for him to begin speaking thus to her: 'I wonder do you feel today / As I have felt . . .' Could he do so, the results might not be as subtle as those in *Two in the Campagna*, but they might also stay closer to reality.

The Bion theme may induce elegy or feeling 'chilly and grown old,' as in *A Toccata of Galuppi's*. Or the contrast may, as often in Browning, be used as a springboard from which to draw implications about the ordained differences between man and the rest of nature. The difficulty in *Love Among the Ruins* is that the dead city belongs to both orders, that is, of humanity and of nature. In death, it seems to have reverted entirely to nature, to have been consumed back into the soil; there were also 'all the men.' Yet Browning could also put into the mouths of his characters the view that the dead should be left to bury their dead: in effect, this is what happens in *By the Fireside*. The fact that the dead so bother the speaker of *Love Among the Ruins*, and of *A Toccata of Galuppi's*, is meant to show something of these speakers' present lives, especially their unprobed or unresolved assumptions. In *By the Fireside* such things are easily disposed of. In *Two in the Campagna* the case is more interesting, for some of the same potential conflict is there, but a resolution is not permitted. Nonetheless the speaker is honest and clear-sighted, and he knows that his answer to what problems the past may have must be found in the present. The whole Bion theme of *A Toccata of Galuppi's* could be developed from the 'Rome and May' of the first stanza. But the *Two in the Campagna* speaker pulls the two conflicting patterns of imagery into relation with his present as shepherd and scientist do not. They remain with the pattern, the shepherd finally altering it to his own needs, the scientist reacting with a mood. The pattern remains unresolved and seems unresolvable. In *Two in the Campagna* the speaker is not subordinated to the pattern. If he cannot trace the spider-thread, neither does it trap him. He sees his alternatives too clearly and returns to his thread too doggedly for that. If his conflict is unresolved, it is not unresolvable—if grace would but descend. He has followed the thread of his thoughts as far as it will lead him: he now needs the confirmation of action. But the other two speakers, as far as we can see, have just grasped the thread.

Sometimes the attitude of Browning's characters is not merely, let the dead bury their dead, but, it is better for them to die. This may be seen in Festus' early speech (Paracelsus later has a very different view of the past):

> Why turn aside from her [wisdom]
> To visit . . . ruins where she paused but would not stay,
> Old ravaged cities that, renouncing her,
> She called an endless curse on, so it came.
>
> (1,404–10)

But the city that is loved can never be so dismissed: 'Beautiful Florence at a word laid low / —(Not in her domes and towers and palaces, / Not even in a dream, that outrage!)' (*Luria*, IV, 259–61). A moment later, Luria, though enraged against Florence, resolves to take as his model the sun, who does not scorch the earth when the earth does not understand him, but simply drops out of the sky, as the sun drops smiling out of the shepherd's day. The closest likeness to the *Love Among the Ruins* setting comes in a later poem, *Aristophanes' Apology*, where Balaustion pictures the destruction of Athens, also a much-loved city, but deserving obliteration:

> Let hill and plain
> Become a waste, a grassy pasture-ground
> Where sheep may wander, grazing goats depend
> From shapeless crags once columns! so at last
> Shall peace inhabit there, and peace enough.
>
> (5535–9)

'The solitary pastures . . . our sheep . . . the hills . . . such peace . . . undistinguished grey': the scenes are very like. May not the shepherd be adopting Balaustion's attitude, assigning the city to the oblivion it merits? But Balaustion has known and loved and fought for her city; she is aware how 'all the men' have betrayed it. More important, she re-creates imaginatively an ideal Athens, which she pictures in the sungilt clouds seen from her fugitive boat; so Sordello also kept an ideal Rome to place against the contemporary one. The problem, to return to familiar Browning categories, is to relate the two. But the shepherd has no second city, only the pastoral landscape and his love-affair; only the city he shuts in, not an aetherial one. He guesses there is some resolution to be found in the present, and he is right. But it will not be found by trying to eliminate the past. This is what Paracelsus tried to do, and concluded finally that he had been scorning the finite. This is what the shepherd also attempts to do: to suppress the achievements of the city, and the question of whether its way of life is really an adequate reason for its being so dead. 'Love is best,' he cries, having gradually eliminated love from his imagined city.

And yet: 'The other day I took up a book two centuries old in which "glory," "soldiering," "rushing to conquer" and the rest, were most thoroughly "believed in"—and if by some miracle the writer had conceived and described some unbeliever, unable to "rush to conquer the Parthians" &c, it would have been as tho' you found a green bough inside a truss of straw' (*LRBEB*, II, 710; Browning to Elizabeth, May 17, 1846; the remark is a propos of 'the Young England imbeciles,' who 'hold that "belief" is the admirable point—*in what*, they judge comparatively immaterial!'). And yet again, on the other side: 'I hear you reproach . . . "their end was a crime."—Oh, a crime will do / As well, I reply, to serve for a test, / As a virtue . . . Let a man contend to the uttermost / For his life's set prize, be it what it will!' The difficulty is, of course, that *Love Among the Ruins* is dramatic. It is not 'proved' one thing or the other by outside references, although these raise pertinent questions about the shepherd's attitudes. Browning in some poems presents arguments very close to those he might have offered in his own person. He also in some poems works out problems close to his own: hunting out the fallacies, showing the consequences of certain positions. The result is that the reader often tends to forget that Browning can and does present attitudes which he is neither for nor against. In *Men and Women* Browning writes some lyrics for which both sympathy and judgment are necessary; in which the dramatic pose is perfectly achieved and maintained. Browning has told us not to read him into these poems. If we cite related lines in other poetry, or remarks in letters, it must be with care. To hear Browning pronouncing 'love is best' is to make of the poem what he tells us not to make. To see the shepherd with some detachment is to recognize that Browning simply leaves him in the contrast of the title—in love among the ruins. To take over the shepherd's categories without seeing how they are shaped and limited robs the poem of much richness. To assume the categories are Browning's own is merely a piece of foolishness, as a glance at other poems shows.

A Toccata of Galuppi's is *Love Among the Ruins* with the terms shifted. Past and present confront each other by means of Galuppi's toccata, which both evokes and judges for a present listener a version of the eighteenth-century Venice in which it was created. Love now belongs not to the present but to the past. Of its quality we know little except that it is emphatically not pastoral arcadian love, and that it inspires a Catullan hyperbole of passion. Galuppi's strictures on it are, on the surface, precisely those of the young shepherd on the buried city, if the sins condemned are different. The speaker is the new element. It is his mind that brings Galuppi alive again, yet he is also spectator to Galuppi's several comments. The first and last stanzas show him detaching himself from the Galuppi world, however, so that a distance is achieved that is not attempted in *Love Among the Ruins*. The dead city and its critic are here seen through the eyes of a third party. His vocation—he is a scientist—makes his detachment appropriate; besides, he is not, like the shepherd, a lover whose love involves him in the dispute at hand.

The most immediate effect of the poem is what its title says it is: a toccata. The rhythm is light (a toccata is a 'touch-piece') but steady and persistent. Its faint beat may hasten or retard or simply accompany the thought, but always regulates it like the quiet ticking of a clock. For a poem in which the passage of time is important, the effect is a happy one. Rhythm suits theme too: no crisis, anguish, vehemence; no crescendos or fortissimos. The first stanza introduces us to the toccata and sets the tempo; it continues until the end, with the last stanza distancing the Venetian picture like the approaching resolution at the music's end. But there is no real resolution. The music approaches its end without affirmation; the clock simply stops and the delicate rhythm is left haunting the air, complete yet cut off. No heavy Weltschmerz can be assigned to 'I feel chilly and grown old'; but the sombre sentiment (like the 'heavy mind' in stanza i) is probably more memorable when in light toccata form than if accompanied by drums and cymbals.

The speaker is a scientist who is also sensitive to musical effect. His role as scientist is not stressed; but it does enable Browning briefly to set up a scene with the scientist trying to 'triumph o'er a secret wrung from nature's close reserve,' but being diverted from his work by Galuppi's haunting music. The music does not mock his work, but raises different questions from those he pursues by avocation—metaphysical questions involving the nature whose secrets he investigates, and questions Browning frequently raised in connection with nature. The scientist has met these questions before. When the poem opens he is retracing their inspiration, as if the toccata is being re-played. Suspense is minimized: we are not experiencing freshly as we do with the shepherd, but repeating an experience whose final effect we know ('But although I take your meaning, 't is with such a heavy mind!'). Theme and rhythm alike will offer no shocks. Yet scientist, like musician, gives the impression of being open-eyed and evading nothing: it is the scientist's business to face facts, including the fact of this kind of question. 'I can hardly misconceive you, it would prove me deaf and blind': Browning's favourite seeing-and-hearing pair are again

used to indicate perception, and the contrast with the shepherd's extin-
guishing of sight and sound comes to mind.

The toccata first re-animates Venice, casually and deftly as the
buried city is first re-animated in *Love Among the Ruins*. 'What, they lived
once thus at Venice . . . ?—and a Venice stereotype springs to life as
readily as Don Juan's dream-Venice. Canals—Shylock—Doge wedding
Adriatic: some explicators of the poem have inferred that the speaker is
unsophisticated because his Venice is a Venice of conventional tourist
landmarks and associations (cf. DeVane, *Handbook*, 221). But the infer-
ence seems to me curious. The speaker sketches a stylized Venice with
stylized inhabitants who all lead a certain sort of life. This is because the
questions Galuppi's music raises do not depend on detailed, close knowledge of eighteenth-century Venetian life—perhaps this is the reason Browning makes the speaker say he has never visited the city. Indeed Galuppi's
music evokes only tentative fancies. The only assertions the speaker
makes are that certain landmarks exist. The rest of the Venetian background is created by questions, tentative interrogations appropriate to the
tentative suggestiveness of the toccata and to its chilly insinuations. It is
true that Browning thought Venetian manners of the time were in general
decadent. It is unlikely that he or this speaker thought every Venetian
behaved like those in the poem, or thought like those in the poem. The
Venetian lovers' first response to the music is not historical: it is precisely
the speaker's own (' "Must we die?" '). Their answer to the question is
different from his—or rather from his lack of an answer, for he simply sees
and feels the question. They lose themselves in each other, like the lovers
among the ruins. The growth and confirmation of the passion that is both
diversion from the question and the lovers' only answer to it is described
in musical terms. It is as if Galuppi both accompanies and directs their
doll-like movements and tender conventionalities—or perhaps as if their
movements and conversation inspire both Galuppi's stylized music and its
ironic questioning. Such interweaving produces considerable irony, always
delicate. The fact that the speaker hears in Galuppi both conventional
Venice and an ironic questioning of even the most conventional Venice
seems to me to show he is far from unsophisticated.

For the speaker reduces his Venetians to their common factor, that
is, the common factor of well-born Venetian grace. I have said that the
Love Among the Ruins speaker is unsophisticated and thinks in stereotypes.
This speaker pictures Venice in stereotypes, but there is no indication he
uses these stereotypes as a basis for judgment. Quite the contrary. He
creates his dead city as the shepherd does, but dispassionately. Its figures
are slight and graceful, its women magnificent, its aspirations simply

personal ones. It is hardly as imposing as the buried city of *Love Among the Ruins*, though this is in large part because of this speaker's detachment. What coincides precisely in the two poems is a moral judgment on an amoral way of life: 'Earth's returns / For whole centuries of folly, noise and sin! . . . Love is best.' ' "Venice spent what Venice earned . . . mirth and folly were the crop: / What of soul was left, I wonder, when the kissing had to stop?" ' But the first heavy-handed moralism is affirmed by the shepherd, the second set aside by the scientist. In *Love Among the Ruins*, Browning refrains from telling us anything about the quality of the shepherd's love; the answers to the poem's questions are not found there. It provides no shadow of an answer, within the poem, to why earth should not also shut in love—with wisdom, silence, goodness, as well as folly, noise, and sin. What I called the Bion theme in that poem is kept under the surface. The shepherd assumes and loudly asserts that his love makes him essentially different from and better than the dead city-dwellers. What earth will return for him, he forbears considering.

In *A Toccata of Galuppi's* the Bion theme is dominant. It is developed through a vegetable-animal imagery that is associated with the Venetians. The Bion theme distinguishes the vegetable and human cycles of nature. The shepherd implies his city-dwellers deserve to be consumed by greedy grass, to be part of the vegetable cycle, while he does not. The scientist is offered by Galuppi the same division between self and past (' "Butterflies may dread extinction,—you'll not die, it cannot be!" '), but refuses such a gambit ('I want the heart to scold. / Dear dead women, with such hair, too—what's become of all the gold / Used to hang and brush their bosoms? I feel chilly and grown old'). Whatever the judgment on souls, this speaker's heart is with the beautiful empty Venetian women.

The vegetable-animal imagery begins with them: 'On her neck the small face buoyant, like a bell-flower on its bed, / O'er the breast's superb abundance where a man might base his head' (it was a bell-flower, a campanula, in which a bee swung when Ottima and Sebald declared their love). The figure here conveys delicacy and movement, together with ampleness and strength, and provides a quick powerful sketch of female allure. But later the image is given other implications: 'As for Venice and her people, merely born to bloom and drop, / Here on earth they bore their fruitage, mirth and folly were the crop.' One effect of the speaker's memorable image at the end of the poem is to transfer the women back from the realm of the bellflower born to bloom and drop, from a vegetable cycle, to a human cycle, or closer to a human cycle. The gold hair yet surviving in their coffins (Browning was to write a poem, *Gold Hair*, on such buried beauty), and remembered as brushing live breasts—such an image affords a certain grief that the flower born to bloom and drop does not.

The parallel animal image to this vegetable one is the butterfly: ' "Butterflies may dread extinction,—you'll not die . . ." ' Whether Browning meant Galuppi's image to remind the reader of the traditional butterfly-psyche association (used, for example, by Jules of Phene's newly awakened soul), I do not know, though I doubt this. If he did, the association would only reinforce the speaker's quiet protest against Galuppi (by implying the Venetians had discernible souls, after all), as well as increasing the irony. Galuppi himself is given the image of the other insect in the poem, a cricket. He is said twice to 'creak' his refrain (the second time sounds like the insect's name: 'so you creak it'), the cricket's persistence having something in common with the toccata's. The cricket is persistent in more ways than one, for he has survived burnt-out Venice: Galuppi's music, once impatiently heard out by flirting Venetians, has outlasted them all. Cricket still creaks while butterfly has flown his brief day. The cricket is given as setting a burned house, so that he can twice echo 'dust and ashes.' The house and phrase pick up the earlier image of intense activity—'balls and masks begun at midnight, burning ever to mid-day'—which is now burnt out. And the phrase, literally applicable to the burnt house, symbolically and chiefly evokes death. It is little wonder that the speaker, hearing the insect's mordant surviving mockery, and remembering the bright gold now entombed in cold earth, himself seems to lose vitality: 'I feel chilly and grown old.'

Man versus nature, or man as a thing of nature; city versus country: what gives shape to some of Browning's finest lyrics can also provide the framework for an irreverent spoof. *Up at a Villa* offers a comic variation on more than one other lyric. In the collected *Dramatic Lyrics*, it follows *Love Among the Ruins* and *A Lovers' Quarrel*, and is followed by *A Toccata of Galuppi's*. Like *Love Among the Ruins* and *A Lovers' Quarrel*, it exhibits an anti-pastoral streak, and like *A Toccata of Galuppi's*, it is a musical poem. By the end we realize that the poem's rhythm is the bang-whang-whang and tootle-te-tootle of the town band in procession as surely as we realize *A Toccata's* rhythm is based on Galuppi. By the end, too, we are likely to opt for country rather than city; as in *Love Among the Ruins*, the monologue has a somewhat different effect from what the speaker intends, though the irony of *Up at a Villa* is of the simplest sort.

The 'quality' of the Italian speaker might be inferred from the first short stanza: a thumping rhythm, stimulating, unavoidable, obvious; repetition (money, money; house, house; such a life, such a life), which simulates the town patter, announces the three focal points of the speaker's concerns, and has the predictable repetition of town life; the point of departure—money; the location of 'such a life'—at the window, as a spectator. None of this needs to be taken very seriously, but it is amusing to see Browning playing variations on persistent imagery of his own. The stance at the window, for example, is not infrequent in Browning and is often significant. Or the speaker avers in the second stanza that the city offers 'something to see, by Bacchus, something to hear, at least'—surely a variation on Browning's favourite seeing-and-hearing pair (here the speaker wants something 'to take the eye' not something the eye takes in).

The circumscription and control of town and houses are obvious, as is the chief threat of the country—its unpredictability. The speaker, being a happy parasite on others' actions, wants the actions to remain controlled, to observe their own due channels so he may safely watch from the shore. Thus the natural in the city is only simulated. The fountain provides a mechanical variation of the dancing stream in *A Lovers' Quarrel*, as do the horses of the wild, leaping horse in the same poem. Even the ladies are contrived: one is the statue in the fountain, who is oblivious to scrutiny of her state of nature (is her weed sash a comic variety of the weed sash at the beginning of the *Purgatorio*, which symbolizes humility?). The other is the 'smiling and smart' (a happy alliterative pair) Mary, in a pink gauze gown 'all spangles,' who is oblivious to seven swords stuck in her heart. Both nymph and virgin have been thoroughly urbanized.

So sure is Browning of his touch, and of this character, that he puts into his mouth one of his most effective natural descriptions, that of the wild tulip shooting up with its 'thin clear bubble of blood.' Of course, it is a weed, and has no business growing among the wheat. And the thin clear bubble of blood has something slightly sinister about it. The Italian dislikes anything so human as blood: when three liberal thieves are shot, it is a news item, not a bloody execution, while a statue of Mary could have any number of swords stuck in her bloodless heart. (Another Italian, a deadly one, also disliked the spot of red summoned all too readily to his last Duchess' cheek.) Children pick and sell the wild tulip, a sylvan picture unlikely to soften the speaker's heart. And the nearness of the sound of 'pick' to 'prick' in following the word "bubble" seems suddenly to deflate the tulip. Nonetheless, Browning does not grant the speaker a second such vivid picture; when he concedes that some think fire-flies pretty, he swiftly adds a reference to stinking hemp.

The clattering rhythm of the processional, '*bang-whang-whang* goes the drum, *tootle-te-tootle* the fife,' is repeated, and the poem closes on it. It is amusing to speculate whether the inspiration for the Italian person of quality might have been Browning's baby son, a devotee of the town, and especially the town band. 'We took a villa a mile and a half from the town, a villa situated on a windy hill (called "poggio al vento"), with magnificent views from all the windows . . .' (*LEB*, I, 458; Sept. 24, 1850). 'We both of us grew rather pathetical on leaving our Sienese villa, and shrank from parting with the pig' (ibid., I, 463; Nov. 13, 1850). 'He [Pen] would change all your trees (except the apple trees), he says, for the Austrian band at any moment. He is rather a town baby . . .' (ibid., I, 458; Sept. [1850]). DeVane identifies the Italian's villa with this 1850 villa of the Brownings from Elizabeth's descriptions to her sisters (*Handbook*, 215), but does not mention Pen as possible source (and mental age?) of the speaker.

Much later, 'bang drum and blow fife' is all the literary critics manage to do (*Pacchiarotto*, 482), a possible retort against the critic who said all Browning's poetry was "bang-whang-whang.' Fife and drum also figure in Don Juan's band; 'Bateleurs, baladines! We shall mot miss the show! / They pace and promenade; they presently will dance: / What good were else i' the drum and fife? O pleasant land of France!' (12–14). The Italian person of quality is a very distant cousin indeed from Don Juan. Still, both are seekers after amusement, if one is very sophisticated; both can glamorize what is shoddy, if one does so knowingly; both are fascinated by a lady in spangles, if one knows the worth of all her glitter. Most important, both are observers not actors, tasters not eaters.

I began this examination of *Men and Women* lyrics by considering enclosure imagery, and the use of one type of such imagery in *Love Among the Ruins* and *A Toccata of Galuppi's* is obvious. At the end of both poems, the living confront the confined dead. For the shepherd, whom they threaten, the dead are to be shut in. For the scientist, whom they move, the dead come briefly alive in strands of long gold hair. But the buried gold of the dead city and of the dead Venetian beauties is equally vanished. Neither speaker offers an alternative strong enough to pull his poem's focus away from the dead, enclosed world that intrigues him. The *Two in the Campagna* speaker does; his poem ends with an impasse, but the focus is on the living man and his pain. Despite his impotence, he is freer than his two fellow-speakers. In both *Love Among the Ruins* and *A Toccata of Galuppi's* it is the dead who prove more vital than the living and who condition the responses of the living.

HAROLD BLOOM

"*Childe Roland*"

The reader, like Browning's belated
quester, might wish to separate origins from aims, but the price of internalization, in poetic as in human romance, is that aims wander back
towards origins. A study of misprision . . . allows the reader to see that
interpretation of Browning's great poem is mocked by the poem itself,
since Roland's monologue is his sublime and grotesque exercise of the
will-to-power over the interpretation of his own text. Roland rides with us
as interpreter; his every interpretation is a powerful misreading; and yet
the union of those misreadings enables him to accept destruction in the
triumphant realization that his ordeal, his trial by landscape, has provided
us with one of the most powerful of texts that any hero-villain since
Milton's Satan has given us.

The poem's opening swerve is marked rhetorically by the trope of
irony, imagistically by an interplay of presence and absence, and psychologically by Roland's reaction-formation against his own destructive impulses. All this is as might be expected, but Browning's enormous skill at
substitution is evident as his poem gets underway, for the strong poet
shows his saving difference from himself as well as others even in his
initial phrases. Roland says one thing and means another, and both the
saying and the meaning seek to void a now intolerable presence. For a
Post-Enlightenment poem to begin, it must know and demonstrate that
nothing is in its right place. Displacement affects at once the precursor
and the poet's own earlier or idealized self, as these were a near-identity.
But the precursor, like the idealized self, does not locate only in the
super-ego or ego ideal. For a poet, both the youth he was and his

From *A Map of Misreading.* Copyright © 1975 by Oxford University Press.

imaginative father reside also in the poetic equivalent of the id. In Romantic quest or internalized romance, an object of desire or even a sublimated devotion to an abstract idea cannot replace the precursor-element in the id, but it does replace the ego ideal, as Freud posited. For Roland, the Dark Tower has been put in the place of the ego ideal of traditional quest, but the obsessed Childe remains haunted by precursor-forces and traces of his own former self in the cramping reaction-formation of his *will-to-fail*, his perverse and negative stance that begins the poem.

Browning asks us to "see Edgar's song in *Lear*" so as to provide an epigraph to go with his poem's title, but I offer instead a sentence from Kierkegaard's *Journals* to serve as Roland's motto:

> The difference between a man who faces death for the sake of an idea and an imitator who goes in search of martyrdom is that whilst the former expresses his idea most fully in death it is the strange feeling of bitterness which comes from failure that the latter really enjoys; the former rejoices in his victory, the latter in his suffering.

(March, 1836)

I think that we can test any interpretation of *Childe Roland to the Dark Tower Came* by this Kierkegaardian distinction. Is Roland finally a hero who faces death for an idea's sake, and if so, for what idea? Or is he, even at the end, what he wills to be at the start and throughout his ride to the Tower, merely an imitator who desires to enjoy the bitterness of failure? Browning is more devious than even Browning could have known, and the great, broken music of the closing stanzas, which *seems* to rejoice in victory, may be only an apotheosis of a poet suffering as poet an apocalyptic consciousness of having failed to become himself. We become great, Kierkegaard always insisted, in proportion to the greatness we fight against, whether that greatness belong to a man, an idea, a system or a poem. Does Roland, at the close, struggle against a greatness, and if so, to whom or what does it belong? How are we to read his poem?

> My first thought was, he lied in every word,
>   That hoary cripple, with malicious eye
>   Askance to watch the working of his lie
> On mine, and mouth scarce able to afford
> Suppression of the glee, that pursed and scored
>   Its edge, at one more victim gained thereby.

Roland's consciousness is grounded in the realization that *meaning has wandered already*, and in a despair at ever bringing it back. "First thought" here is not opposed to a second or later thought, which actually never enters the poem, and so "first thought" itself is an irony or the beginning of one. For Roland indeed is saying one thing while meaning another, and what he means is that the cripple inevitably speaks the truth. I take pleasure, retrospectively, having published a less advanced reading of this poem earlier (in *The Ringers in the Tower*, 1971) in now finding a critical precursor in the formidable Mrs. Sutherland Orr. That strong-minded disciple of Browning anticipated Betty Miller, George Ridenour and myself in her acute suspicions of Roland's reliability:

> So far the picture is consistent; but if we look below its surface discrepancies appear. The Tower is much nearer and more accessible than Childe Roland has thought; a sinister-looking man, of whom he asked the way, and who, as he believed, was deceiving him, has really put him on the right track; and as he describes the country through which he passes, it becomes clear that half its horrors are created by his own heated imagination.

But the third stanza shows that Roland never believed the cripple was deceiving him, since in it Roland speaks of "that ominous tract which, *all agree*, hides the Dark Tower," the tract being where the cripple directed him. Still, Mrs. Orr came close to the right interpretative principle, which is to be fairly suspicious of everything Roland says, and highly suspicious of nearly everything he says he sees, at least until his final vision.

On the model of the map of misprision, *Childe Roland* is a poem in three parts: stanzas I–VIII, IX–XXIX, XXX–XXXIV. Stanzas I–VIII are the induction, during which an initial contraction or withdrawal of meaning is gradually redressed by a substitution or representation of the quest. Rhetorically, irony yields to synecdoche, psychologically a reaction-formation gives way to a turning-against-the-self, and imagistically a total sense of absence is replaced by a restituting sense of some partial significance, with a larger representation, a lost wholeness, still kept in abeyance:

> Thus, I had so long suffered in this quest,
> Heard failure prophesied so oft, been writ
> So many times among "The Band"—to wit,
> The knights who to the Dark Tower's search addressed
> Their steps—that just to fail as they, seemed best,
> And all the doubt was now—should I be fit?

A desire that one be fit to fail—though this is a reversal of quest, is yet an advance on the poem's opening, an antithetical completion of that ironic swerve from origins. Any quest is a synecdoche for the whole of desire; a quest for failure is a synecdoche for suicide. What is unique to the figurations of the first part of Browning's poem is Roland's twisted pride in his own sense of election to "The Band" of questers. This rhetorical first movement ends with stanza VIII:

> So, quiet as despair, I turned from him,
>> That hateful cripple, out of his highway
>> Into the path he pointed. All the day
> Had been a dreary one at best, and dim
> Was settling to its close, yet shot one grim
>> Red leer to see the plain catch its estray.

"Estray" is founded on *extra* + *vagare*, to wander beyond limits or out of the right way. Roland is an estray, a hyperbolic wanderer, whose dominant trait is extravagance, the Binswangerian *Verstiegenheit*, the state of having climbed to a height from which one cannot descend safely. The "grim red leer" of the sunset marks the transition to the poem's second movement (IX–XXIX), its ordeal-by-landscape.

This sequence of stanzas alternates between the psychic defense of isolation and the more Sublime defense of repression, but collapsed here into the Grotesque:

> Then came a bit of stubbed ground, once a wood,
>> Next a marsh, it would seem, and now mere earth
>> Desperate and done with; (so a fool finds mirth,
> Makes a thing and then mars it, till his mood
> Changes and off he goes!) within a rood—
>> Bog, clay and rubble, sand and stark black dearth.
>
> Now blotches rankling, coloured gay and grim,
>> Now patches where some leanness of the soil's
>> Broke into moss or substances like boils;
> Then came some palsied oak, a cleft in him
> Like a distorted mouth that splits its rim
>> Gaping at death, and dies while it recoils.

This landscape is a landscape of repetition, but in the deadliest sense, one in which all questions of genesis have yielded to mere process, to one-thing-after-another. Here, in the long middle part of Browning's poem, one is in a world of contiguities, in which resemblances, if they manifest themselves at all, must be grotesque. Roland describes his landscape like Zola describing an urban scene, yet Roland's world is wholly visionary, its "realism" a pure self-imposition. Roland's landscape is a kind of continuous metonymy, in which a single, negative aspect of every thing substitutes for the thing itself. When the dialectic of restitution seeks to operate in this middle part of the poem, it substitutes for this emptying-out-by-isolation with a hyperbolic vision of the heights; yet this is a nightmare Sublime:

For, looking up, aware I somehow grew,
    'Spite of the dusk, the plain had given place
    All round to mountains—with such name to grace
Mere ugly heights and heaps now stolen in view.
How thus they had surprised me,—solve it, you!
    How to get from them was no clearer case.

Repression, even if unconscious, is still a purposeful process, and the reader can solve the "how" of Roland's being surprised, by an awareness of the characteristic workings of repression. Roland has forgotten (on purpose) or willed (in his depths) not to be aware of both an inward impulse (suicidal self-punishment) and an outer event (the failure of his precursors in "The Band"), both of which tempt him towards yielding to instinctual demands that his ego-ideal finds objectionable. These demands would merge him into his landscape of dearth, and can be termed nihilistic, in the full and uncanny sense best defined by Nietzsche. Roland too would rather have the void as purpose than be void of purpose, yet his wayward impulses court every evidence of purposelessness. For Roland, despite his overt allegiance to his Band of precursors, is a revisionist strong poet, and so a hero-villain, even of and in his own poem. His misprision or mis-taking of his inherited quest-pattern culminates in stanza XXIX, which ends the second movement of the poem:

Yet half I seemed to recognize some trick
    Of mischief happened to me, God knows when—
    In a bad dream perhaps. Here ended, then,
Progress this way. When, in the very nick
Of giving up, one time more, came a click
    As when a trap shuts—you're inside the den!

In the nick or crucial moment of giving up, which would be the prolongation of a wholly negative repetition, Roland is suddenly startled into a climactic recognition, which is that he is trapped, yet paradoxically this entrapment alone makes possible a fulfillment of his quest. Just here, before the poem proceeds to its final movement, the problem of interpretation is most difficult. The meaning of *Childe Roland to the Dark Tower Came* is most problematic in its last five stanzas, which alternate between an *askesis* of defeated metaphor and a magnificent, perhaps triumphant metaleptic return of earlier powers.

What are we to make of Roland's perspectivism, his metaphoric juxtapositions between inside and outside?

Burningly it came on me all at once,
    This was the place! those two hills on the right,

Crouched like two bulls locked horn in horn in fight;
While to the left, a tall scalped mountain . . . Dunce,
Dotard, a-dozing at the very nonce,
After a life spent training for the sight!

Metaphors for art as an activity tend to center upon a particular place, where a heightened sense of presence can manifest itself. This is a place, as Hartman says, both of heightened demand and of an intensified consciousness that attempts to meet such demand by an increased power of representation. Browning's Roland, exultantly proclaiming: "This was the place!" brings together most of the crucial variants of the metaphor for art as an activity. Roland confronts at once a staged scene, a court of judgment (his failed precursors in "The Band"), and, most heroically, an initiation, a purgatorial induction parallel to that of Keats in *The Fall of Hyperion* or Shelley in *The Triumph of Life*. Part of the resonance, the strong sense of inevitability, in the next stanza, is due to Browning's perfect choice of the Dark Tower as the ultimate metaphor for art's Scene of Instruction:

What in the midst lay but the Tower itself?
The round squat turret, blind as the fool's heart,
Built of brown stone, without a counterpart
In the whole world. The tempest's mocking elf
Points to the shipman thus the unseen shelf
He strikes on, only when the timbers start.

Shall we, tentatively, call both the Dark Tower and the mocking elf the Oedipal necessities of self-betrayal in the practice of art? Or, more narrowly, the Tower and the elf are metaphors for misprision, for the over-determined and inescapable meanings that belated creators impose upon poetic tradition. The Tower stands for the blindness of the influence-process, which is the same as the reading-process. Fresh creation is a catastrophe, or a substitution, a making-breaking that is performed in blindness. The elf mocks by pointing to the unseen hazard "only when the timbers start," which is after the new poem has been begotten by blindness upon blindness. Roland is giving us a parable of his relation to his brother-knights, which becomes a parable of Browning's relation to the poets who quested for the Dark Tower before him.

The Tower *is* Dark because it stands for the possibilities and therefore also the limitations of metaphor as such, which means for the blindness of all inside/outside perspectivisms. The paradox of perspectivism . . . is that it depends wholly on the subject/object dualism, while attempting to be a way of seeing more clearly. It is not accidental that the greatest perspectivist in poetry is Milton's Satan, for the effect of an absolute perspectivism is to bring about a subjective dissolving of all knowledge, and so an ebbing away of the distinction between factual truth and falsity. As much as the tautologies of the solipsist, the perspectivism of Satan (or of Roland) is necessarily self-contradictory. The Dark Tower lay in the midst, but for Roland there can be no "midst"; and his inability to see the Tower as such, after a lifetime training for the sight, is enormously instructive.

But Browning, and Roland, do not end with limiting and so with failed metaphor:

> Not see? because of night perhaps—why, day
>   Came back again for that! before it left,
>   The dying sunset kindled through a cleft:
> The hills, like giants at a hunting, lay,
> Chin upon hand, to see the game at bay,—
>   "Now stab and end the creature—to the heft!"
>
> Not hear? when noise was everywhere! it tolled
>   Increasing like a bell. Names in my ears
>   Of all the lost adventurers my peers,—
> How such a one was strong, and such was bold,
> And such was fortunate, yet each of old
>   Lost, lost! one moment knelled the woe of years.

These stanzas, together with the last one, which follows them, constitute a transumptive scheme or figure of a figure, which undoes the figurative assertions of Roland throughout the entire poem before them. Roland is belated, the last of the Band, and yet of his belatedness he now makes (and breaks) an earliness, at the apparent expense of his life. The act of representation here is both proleptic, foretelling a future that lies just beyond the span of the poem, and "preposterous," inverting the quest-pattern by revealing the past failures as being something other than failures. What are we to interpret Roland's "day came back again for that!" as meaning? Realistically, it may tell us that Roland's time-sense in the long middle part of the poem is a delusion, for "the dying sunset kindled" may be identical with the "red leer" of the sun at the end of stanza VIII. Whether that is so, or whether the last kindling of sunset is a kind of lapse in nature, either way Roland is troping upon and so undoing an earlier trope. He thus calls attention to the rhetoricity of his closing statement by raising both his own word-consciousness and that of his reader, in a manner rather akin to Nietzsche's in *Zarathustra*. His rhetorical questions "Not see?" and "Not hear?" become hyperboles of hyperboles, and place the poem's previously grotesque sublimities in considerable doubt. What he *sees* is the place of trial, scene of his true ordeal, which is not to be by landscape, but by the return to his precursors. What he *hears* are the celebrated names of the precursors and the cause for the celebration, strength and loss tolling together in one increasing dirge. What remains is vision proper, as the once-ruined quester is transformed into a seer. Where earlier we distrusted everything Roland told us he saw, now we see feelingly all that he tells:

> There they stood, ranged along the hill-sides, met
>> To view the last of me, a living frame
>> For one more picture! in a sheet of flame
> I saw them and I knew them all. And yet
> Dauntless the slug-horn to my lips I set,
>> And blew. "*Childe Roland to the Dark Tower came.*"

The perspectivism of the Dark Tower metaphor has been overcome by that final line, where the Childe presents himself as the limner of his own night-piece, the poet rather than the subject of his poem. The precursor-questers meet to view the last of Roland, as an outside to his inside, but he has attained what Yeats was to call the Condition of Fire, and in that flame he views the last of them, and unlike them he both sees and *knows* what he sees. Because he has attained knowledge and is transformed, they no longer know him. Undefeated by his total knowledge, he abandons the world of romance and enters prophecy, by setting the slug-horn of the tragic, suicidal, too-early Romantic poet Chatterton to his lips. What he blows is his poem, as we have to read it, the trumpet of a prophecy because of its transumptive relation to Romantic prophecy.

So far we have read *Childe Roland* as a revisionary text, on the model of our map of misprision. But on the larger model of our Scene of Instruction . . . this is only the first level of interpretation (the rhetorical, psychological and imagistic one) in the hierarchy of how to read a poem. We need to ask next: What is the interpretation of tradition, and in particular of the central precursor or precursors, that this poem's revisionary ratios give us? Moving up our ladder of interpretation, we then will contrast the Word brought forward by the later poet with the rival Word of his father. Next we will climb to a contrast of rival inspirations or muses, and beyond that to a consideration of the Covenant-love between the two poets, or more simply, the pact explicit or implicit that the latecomer makes with the earlier poet. Finally, we will consider the Election-love between the poets, that is to say, why the later poet felt himself Chosen or found by the earlier poet, and what difference that made in his sense of vocation.

It is important to notice that so far I have excluded from this discussion virtually all consideration of the poetic tradition that formed Browning, as well as an account of Browning's relation to a specific precursor, and also what generally would be termed the "sources" of *Childe Roland to the Dark Tower Came.* My motive is to distinguish once for all what I call "poetic influence" from traditional "source study." Antithetical criticism as a practical discipline of reading begins with an analysis of misprision or revisionism, through a description of revisionary ratios, conducted through examination of tropes, imagery or psychological defenses, depending upon the preferences of an individual reader. An application of literary history, though greatly desirable, is not strictly necessary for the study of misprision. But as soon as one attempts a deeper criticism, and asks what is the interpretation that a poem offers, one is involved with the precursor text or texts as well as with the belated poem itself.

Shelley is the Hidden God of the universe created by *Childe Roland to the Dark Tower Came.* His is the presence that the poem labors to void, and his is the force that rouses the poem's force. Out of that struggle between forces rises the form of Browning's poem, which is effectively the *difference* between the rival strengths of poetic father and poetic son. I would agree with Paul de Man that all strong poems contain an authentically self-negating element, a genuinely epistemological moment, but always I would insist that this moment comes in *their relationship to a prior poem,* a relationship that remains inescapably subject-to-subject centered. In *Childe Roland,* this moment is reserved for the end, for the final stanza. There Roland negates the larger part of his poem, a negation that strengthens rather than weakens the poem, because there Roland suffers a unique act of knowledge, an act that clarifies both his personal past and tradition, though at the expense of both presence and the present. By "presence" I mean both Roland's self-presence, and also the virtual existence of any opposing force in the poem other than Roland's internalization of the precursors.

Let me offer an explicit, indeed a reductive and therefore simplified total interpretation of the poem, firmly based on the model of misprision I have been tracing. There is no ogre at or in the Dark Tower for Roland to confront; the Tower is windowless and uninhabited, as blind as Roland's own fool's heart. "Fool" as a word goes back to the Latin *follis* for "bellows," and so a fool originally was a windbag. The root *bhel* means to blow or swell, which gives a triumphant twist to Roland's final act of blowing his slug-horn. In the *Song of Roland* this act is a signal to Roland's friends and is at the expense of almost the last breath of the mortally wounded hero. But Childe Roland's friends are disgraced and dead, and only the Childe's heart has been wounded, by the blind foolishness of questing for failure. Yet we feel, as readers, that death or at least mortal combat must be at hand as the poem ends. If Roland is alone at the end, as he is throughout the poem, then who is the antagonist? Certainly not "The Band" of brothers and precursors, for they stand ranged in vision, at the close. They may be a court in judgment, but they are there to see and to be seen, not to act.

There is only Roland himself to serve both as hero and as villain, only Roland to sound the trumpet as warning against Roland. The Childe stands in judgment against his own antithetical quest and, however lovingly, against his antithetical precursors as well. His blast on the slug-horn is an interpretation of his precursors' quest, which is to say that the poem becomes Browning's interpretation of a poem like Shelley's *Ode to the West Wind,* and perhaps of all Shelley's poetry. Roland sees himself at last as what he is, the solitary poet-quester, the *penseroso* so dangerously internalized as to have become anti-natural or antithetical, a counter-placing figure who stands against all the continuities that make life possible for the natural man. Roland is the culmination, akin to Tennyson's Ulysses, of the development undergone by his immediate ancestors: Wordsworth's Solitary in *The Excursion,* Byron's Childe Harold, Shelley's poet-wanderer in *Alastor* and in *Prince Athanase.* One can recall the lines by Shelley in his *Athanase* fragment that perpetually haunted Yeats:

> His soul had wedded Wisdom, and her dower
> Is love and justice, clothed in which he sate
> Apart from men, as in a lonely tower,
> Pitying the tumult of their dark estate.

Roland's tower is closer to the less idealized tower of Shelley's *Julian and Maddalo:*

> I looked, and saw between us and the sun
> A building on an island; such a one
> As age to age might add, for uses vile,
> A windowless, deformed and dreary pile;
> And on the top an open tower, where hung
> A bell, which in the radiance swayed and swung;
> We could just hear its hoarse and iron tongue:
> The broad sun sunk behind it, and it tolled
> In strong and black relief.

We can juxtapose to this a passage from Browning's *Essay on Shelley,* where Browning portrays himself as he would have been, a dramatic or "objective" poet rather than a Shelleyan "subjective" poet like Roland:

Did the personality of such an one stand like an open watchtower in the midst of the territory it is erected to gaze on . . . ? Or did some sunken and darkened chamber of imagery witness . . . how rare and precious were the outlooks through here and there an embrasure upon a world beyond . . . ?

Roland has come, not to an open watch-tower, whether of Athanase's or Browning's "objective" poet, but to the madhouse of *Julian and Maddalo.* His solipsism, sustained to the ultimate "realism" of his ordeal-by-landscape, would be total and therefore a madness if it were not for his final vision of his precursors, a vision that saves his sense of otherness and so still gives him purposiveness, thus bestowing meaning upon his last act. Yet the phantasmagoria of his final quest was due to his horror of the past, his dread of failing as his precursors failed, a dread that nevertheless became the sympathetic antipathy (as Kierkegaard called his concept of Dread) that motivated his quest. Roland has triumphed by failing precisely as his precursors failed, and by recognizing and so *knowing* that their "failure" was a triumph also. Each one in turn found himself alone at the Dark Tower, facing himself as opponent at the Scene of Instruction, measuring himself always against the composite form of the forerunners. The Dark Tower is the self-negating element in the activity of art, and Roland is the poetic consciousness at its most dangerous to itself and to all others, burning through nature and so through everything in the self that is not the imagination.

As misprision, *Childe Roland to the Dark Tower Came* means the interplay of tropes, defenses, images that we have been studying. As *lidrosh*, interpretation, it means a de-idealizing critique of Shelley, but a wholly loving critique, one that exposes not the generous power of Shelley's trumpet of a prophecy, but something more of the experiential cost than the remorselessly noble Shelley would deign to acknowledge. As a Word of Browning's own brought forward, *Childe Roland* contrasts with Shelley's less psychologically revealing word, for Browning is a congeries of persons, and Shelley much more of a single being. Where the inspiration of Shelley is Orphic, Browning's is more unconditioned and absolute, because closer both to solipsism and to madness. The covenant between Shelley and Browning calls for a refusal to compromise with anything not in itself solitary and imaginative, and this covenant Browning has broken, with a consequent guilt present throughout Roland's monologue. But the Election-love burns on fiercely in Browning's Condition of Fire, as it will in Yeats's, for the sense of vocation in Roland as in Browning is renewed perpetually by Shelley's uncompromising and so both inspiring and chiding example. A more total reading of *Childe Roland* than I have space for here would mount up through all these contrasts.

But something of the conclusion can be surmised here, however tentatively. Roland's equivocal triumph is an instance of Kierkegaardian "repetition" rather than of Platonic "recollection" or Hegelian "mediation," if only because the Romantic trope-upon-a-trope or transumption leads to a projective or introjective stance of which Kierkegaard is the conscious anti-Platonic and anti-Hegelian theorist. Precisely what Roland refuses is the Golgotha of Absolute Spirit that Hegel proclaims at the very close of his *Phenomenology*:

> Knowledge is aware not only of itself, but also of the negative of itself, or its limit. Knowing its limit means knowing how to sacrifice itself. This sacrifice is . . . self-abandonment. . . . Here it has to begin all over again at its immediacy, as freshly as before, and thence rise once more to the measure of its stature, as if, for it, all that preceded were lost, and as if it had learned nothing from the experience of the spirits that preceded. But re-collection has conserved that experience, and is the inner being, and, in fact, the higher form of the substance. While, then, this phase of Spirit begins all over again its formative development, apparently starting solely from itself, yet at the same time it commences at a higher level. The realm of spirits developed in this way, and assuming definite shape in existence, constitutes a succession, where one detaches and sets loose the other, and each takes over from its predecessor the empire of the spiritual world.

Against this high idealism of what is essentially the influence-process, we can set one of Kierkegaard's central insights:

> It requires youth to hope, and youth to recollect, but it requires courage to will repetition. . . . For hope is an alluring fruit which does not satisfy, recollection is a miserable pittance which does not satisfy, but repetition is the daily bread which satisfies with benediction. When one has circumnavigated existence, it will appear whether one has courage to understand that life is a repetition, and to delight in that very fact. . . . Repetition is reality, and it is the seriousness of life.

From Hegel we can move to Mallarmé's *Igitur,* and an illuminating observation by Paul de Man, even as from Kierkegaard we can go back to *Childe Roland* and the critical mode I endeavor to develop. Meditating on *Igitur,* de Man remarks that in Baudelaire and in Mallarmé (under Baudelaire's influence) "ennui" is no longer a personal feeling but comes from the burden of the past. A consciousness comes to know itself as negative and finite. It sees that others know themselves also in this way, and so it transcends the negative and finite present by seeing the universal nature of what it itself is becoming. So de Man says of Mallarmé's view, comparing it to Hegel's, that "we develop by dominating our natural anxiety and alienation and by transforming it in the awareness and the knowledge of otherness."

The difference between Hegel and Kierkegaard is also a difference between Mallarmé and Browning, as it happens, and critically a difference between a deconstructive and an antithetical view of practical criticism. Kierkegaard's "repetition" is closer than its Hegelian rival (or the Nietzschean-Heideggerian descendant) to the mutually exploitative relationships between strong poets, a mutuality that affects the dead nearly as much as the living. Insofar as a poet authentically is and remains a poet, he must exclude and negate other poets. Yet he must begin by including and affirming a precursor poet or poets, for there is no other way to become a poet. We can say then that a poet is *known as* a poet only by a wholly contradictory including/excluding, negating/affirming which by the agency of psychic defenses manifests as an introjecting/projecting. "Repetition," better even than Nietzsche's Eternal Return of the Same, is what rhetorically manifests itself through the scheme of transumption, where the surrender of the present compensates for the contradictory movements of the psyche.

Roland is not mediated by his precursors; they do not detach him from history so as to free him in the spirit. The Childe's last act of dauntless courage is to will repetition, to accept his place in the company of the ruined. Roland tells us implicitly that the present is not so much negative and finite as it is willed, though this willing is never the work of an individual consciousness acting by itself. It is caught up in a subject-to-subject dialectic, in which the present moment is sacrificed, not to the energies of art, but to the near-solipsist's tragic victory over himself. Roland's negative moment is neither that of renunciation nor that of the loss of self in death or error. It is the negativity that is self-knowledge yielding its power to a doomed love of others, in the recognition that those others, like Shelley, had more grandly surrendered knowledge and its powers to love, however illusory. Or, most simply, Childe Roland dies, if he dies, in the magnificence of a belatedness that can accept itself as such. He ends in strength, because his vision has ceased to break and deform the world, and has begun to turn its dangerous strength upon its own defenses. Roland is the modern poet-as-hero, and his sustained courage to weather his own phantasmagoria and emerge into fire is a presage of the continued survival of strong poetry.

ANN WORDSWORTH

Browning's Anxious Gaze

In *On Heroes, Hero-worship and the Heroic in History*, Carlyle writes "Poetic creation—what is this too but *seeing* the thing sufficiently—the Word that will describe the thing follows of itself from such clear intense sight of the thing. The seeing eye—it is this that discloses the inner harmony of things. To the poet, as to every other, we say, first of all, *see*." Browning agrees, for he writes to Joseph Milsand about his volume *Men and Women*: "I am writing . . . lyrics with more music and painting in them than before so as to get people to hear and see."

And yet, this act of seeing which Carlyle acclaimed so confidently, how uncannily it manifests itself if one rejects an idealist account of its nature in favour of a psychoanalytical one: how quickly then "the inner harmony of things" dissolves, once the matchings of a reflexive consciousness are no longer assumed. For what Carlyle's directive takes for granted are two notions which psychoanalytical theory rejects: the presence of a unified consciousness and the primacy of representation. And this in itself might make one want to reconsider the critical commonplaces that take too easily this matter of making people see.

Browning's work so hauntingly calls for a more subtle reading than falls to his lot as purveyor of experience—and yet could the dramatic monologues be discussed at all without assuming "a literature of empiricism"? Is it possible to account for their success and the pleasure they provide without the expected appeal to empathy and identification? More precisely, is it possible to draw in a psycho-aesthetics, Lacan's account of

From *Robert Browning: A Collection of Critical Essays*, edited by Harold Bloom and Adrienne Munich. Copyright © 1979 by Ann Wordsworth. Prentice-Hall, Inc.

"the pacifying Apollonian effect of painting," and coordinate it with Harold Bloom's theory of poetry, the relation of influence and the revisionary processes—that is, to use two accounts of creative effects that take scant heed of the categories of perception and experience?

According to Bloom, the hardest thing in reading Browning is to distinguish the literal from the figurative and vice versa. So it is obvious that this matter of getting people to see turns on more than a heightened sense of vision and a tapping of experiential wisdom. How fortunate then that one of Lacan's most interesting seminars, *Of the Gaze as Objet Petit a,* should be on the scopic drive and that this should show how the gaze, the relation of desire, structures the visual field beyond the organizations of the conscious system.

It is the factitiousness of the analytic experience that Lacan's work centres on, its indifference to relations of truth and appearance. "In our relation to things, insofar as this relation is constituted by the way of vision and ordered in figures of representation, something slips, passes, is transmitted from stage to stage and is always to some degree eluded in it—that is what we call the gaze." This drift is not accounted for in theories of geometral vision; for they do no more than map space, and contain so little of the scopic itself that, as Diderot proves, this mapping can be reconstructed without loss for the touch of a blind man. Anamorphosis, the disarrangement of geometral space by a skewed perspective, shows more of what is missed by the reflexive consciousness; hence the power of the anamorphic object in Holbein's painting *The Ambassadors,* where the viewer is shown his own eclipse as he turns back to see the enigmatic shape as a human skull. However, it is not the presence of symbols which organizes the field of the visible, but the gaze itself, which does not only look but also *shows*—that is, forms as desire like the dream (itself a gratuitous showing), and situates the perceiver where he cannot any longer say "After all, I am the consciousness of this. . . ."

There is another dislocation; unconscious desire is not humanized. Lacan makes this clear when he is questioned at the end of a seminar, "When you relate psychoanalysis to Freud's desire and to the desire of the hysteric, might you not be accused of psychologism?" Lacan's answer is that there is no original subjectivity at stake: desire is an object in the unconscious functioning, and not to be confused with events and relationships in biographical life. So it is never a matter of relating creative processes to psychobiographical details—unless perhaps to show a blurring of the process by unmanageable biographical material, as, say, in *The Professor* or *Oliver Twist.*

So, art and the spectator, art and artists, are bounded neither by the empirical relations of geometral space nor by shared subjectivities, but, according to Lacan, by the field of the scopic drive—a field orientated by the eye, whose appetite the painting feeds, and which is satisfied not by representations but by what Lacan calls the *trompe-l'oeil* and the *dompte-regard*, the lure and the taming of the gaze. The first, which in poetry might be the lure of *its* representations (in Browning, "Men and Women"), satisfies and attracts, not because of its fidelity to experience, but because through the pretence of representation we glimpse our relation to the unconscious. When Plato protests against the deception of art, his contention is not that painting gives an illusory equivalence to the object. "The painting does not compete with appearance, it competes with what Plato designates for us beyond appearance as being the Idea." What solicits us in painting is shown quite boldly in the pleasure given by a technical *trompe-l'oeil*—that moment of shifted focus when the illusion does not move with the eye, when it vanishes as what it feigned and emerges as something else not subject to appearance, in Lacanian terms, the "objet petit a," the unrepresentable object of desire. And this relation between *trompe-l'oeil* and *objet a* could also be the unconscious structuration beyond the slide of literal and figurative in Browning's poetry, the troping movement which Bloom shifts across the formal divisions of grammar and rhetoric into the revisionary processes, the interplay of rhetorical, psychological and imagistic moves which constitutes poetic energy. If the lure of art, its allure, is this glimpsing, then it accompanies the intra-poetic relations that Bloom describes by the uncanny dissolution of precursor-poet into *objet a*: unconscious and formal processes merge under the auspices of a seeing eye, though not indeed as Carlyle intended.

The other move that Lacan describes, the *dompte-regard*, the taming of the gaze, is the *showing* that gratifies the appetite of the eye; yet this also has no reference to representation, for it is not an optical pleasure that is described. As it functions in relation to the unconscious, the eye is voracious, possessed by *invidia*, the envy exemplified by St. Augustine as he gazed on his brother at his mother's breast: "the envy that makes the subject pale before the image of a completeness closed upon itself, before the idea that the *petit a*, the separated *a* from which he is hanging, may be for another the possession that gives satisfaction." The pacifying effect of art is that it permits the laying down of this gaze by its recognition of the eye's desire. As if the painter said—how different his tone from Carlyle's— "You want to see. Well, take a look at this. . . ." And this effect, which Lacan calls "the taming, civilizing and fascinating power of the function of the picture," is what has never been well described before, the Freudian sublimation. Might it not be found also in the assuagement of the vora-cious unrest which marks creative anxiety, in the poet's power to acknowl-edge desire and lack in the formulations of poet-and-precursor?

There is one more move in this seminar *Of the Gaze* which can be drawn in. Critics insist on Browning's power to think himself into charac-ter and events—indeed this virtuosity is seen as his main achievement ("one's normal processes of judgment are well nigh suspended and one emerges from the experiences of the poem dazzled by the illusion of having actually penetrated an alien being and a remote period of history," as J. W. Harper puts it). To settle the question of how the subject places himself within the scopic field, Lacan uses the analogy of mimicry. This is not simply a matter of adaptation—that is, behaviour as bound up with survival means—but a series of functions manifesting themselves outside any biologistic explanation. Travesty, camouflage, intimidation, all have structural and psychic implications. "All reveal something in so far as it is distinct from what might be called an *itself* that is behind" camouflage, the production of the background; travesty, the breaking up of being between itself and its semblance; intimidation, the extension of being by overvalu-ation. All the moves suggest that imitation is not a faithful representa-tion, but rather the subject's involuntary insertion within an unconscious function. The parallel between mimicry and art is taken for granted by Roger Caillois, whose work Lacan quotes; it is used with more reserve by Lacan himself. But here too there are implications for Browning criticism. If mimicry (travesty, camouflage, intimidation) were embodied in the representations of the dramatic monologues, Browning would be screened from the full play of influence anxiety while still inscribing the poet-precursor relation within the poems. Character and events would no longer be transcriptions of experience but signs of a defensive energy—a creative play that slips, passes and eludes capture altogether as representation.

The difficulty by now, of course, is obvious enough: the factitious-ness of Lacanian description could hardly be further from the robust pleasures of recognition that Browning's readers expect. Instead of the assurance of a heightened vision, there is only a glimpse of processes so obscure that consciousness has no sense of them. But there are advantages in such a reading. The narrative ingenuities that are so admired soon pall and yet critics are still ready to accept tacitly Oscar Wilde's verdict: "Yes, Browning was great. And as what will he be remembered? As a poet? Ah, not as a poet. He will be remembered as a writer of fiction, as the most supreme writer of fiction, it may be, that we have ever had." No matter, it seems, that Wilde's assumptions about fiction ("men and women that live") go unquestioned, and that this in its turn presupposes a neglect of

Browning's early poetry and a simplistic account of his poetic development (an overall movement from the confessional Shelleyan monodramas to the achieved objectivity of the later poems after a radical break in 1842). In place of this, it is surely possible to suggest the presence of creative processes which form around the obsessive preoccupations of the belated poet and which gain power from the transindividual linking of art and unconscious functioning. And this would mean questioning idealist accounts of poetic language (its unique power to match human consciousness), although substantiating its indifferent and inexhaustible energies. If the monologues are not as Wilde describes them, supreme fictions, but rather fictive substitutions, *trompe-l'oeil* displacements of creative lack and desire, then reading them would involve a slide away from representations and a recognition of a mimicry whose relation is with the envy of the scopic drive, with the *objet a* reformed as the precursor. This process centres formally in the play between literal and figurative; its material is not just the historic figure, the event but the use of these representations as displacements—richly dramatised effects behind whose *trompe l'oeil* are glimpsed the figurations of desire and lack condensed as the relation to the precursor.

How is this shown? All the monologues at first reading seem like anecdotes, held together by solid figures, animated by a plot with ironic undertones and psychological nuances. My *Last Duchess*: the subject seems so clearly and movingly apparent, disturbing only in the ambivalence the reader feels through his own admiration of the Duke's style. Surely then, it is just a matter of seeing how the dramatic irony works out, of making a choice such as is offered, say, in *The Browning Critics*—a choice between Browning's witless Duke and Browning's shrewd Duke?

If one no longer centres on the referents, the characters, but tries to reconstitute the other scene, then a very different movement emerges—a beautifully complex play on the obsessive themes that haunt the creative mind, chiefly *invidia*, the fear, anger and avenges of influence anxiety. Ostensibly, the clash in the poem is between life and art—the warmth and carnal beauty of the woman and her subjection to the Duke's murderous fantasy. But behind this lies the relation of poet and precursor, doubly disguised insomuch as the precariousness of the belated poet is masked as a helpless subjection to critical misjudgements; in effect, J. S. Mill's critical misreading of *Pauline* stands in as a cover for Browning's misprision of *Alastor*. At the narrative level the poem can seize a triumph over the tyrannies that master it. The Duke intends the listening envoy to judge his last Duchess as he does, but her erotic charm escapes his description and we see her not as the mute victim of his fantasies but in her own involuntary triumph over them. Nevertheless anxiety is in the poem too. The figurations are entirely unstable and shift from level to level as literal narrative, compensatory fantasy, representations of psychic processes. Though the Duchess is obliterated, her presence hauntingly survives, figuring indifferently as poetic victory over detractors, or as precursor, negated but still active. The poem plays on the aporia between literal and figurative, in a nonrelational movement whose enigmatic activity is beautifully idealised by who but Shelley in *The Defence of Poetry:*

> The mind in creation is a fading coal which some invisible influence like an inconstant wind awakens to transitory brightness; this power arises from within, like the colours of a flower which fades and changes as it is developed, and the conscious portions of our nature are unprophetic either of its approach or of its departure.

The Duke unintentionally allows a presence to revive; whereas all he meant to do was draw back a curtain, show a picture, lift a shroud. And amidst the poem Shelley's fading coal is ablaze again—indifferently, as the presence of the precursor, as the *objet a,* whatever it is that tames and allures in the pulsations of literal and figurative, that is, in poetry.

In the monodramas, direct dramatizations of creative experience, this play is not made; but it is in the two poems *Porphyria's Lover* and *Johannes Agricola in Meditation,* first printed in Fox's *Monthly Repository,* January 1836, six years before the supposed break. In *Porphyria's Lover,* the play of substitutions moves from the narrative surface of character and macabre action to another secret act of violence. By murder the lover transforms his wayward mistress into his puppet-doll—so too would the poet reduce his precursor. But barbarous action is only one part of the poem, the surface logic of a jealous panic, casting its power over the defiant resistancies of sexuality and of the master poem. Under this is the mimicking—a blackly comic play of the creative mind, shuffling and redealing the cards of our mortality time, change, age, infidelity, death. When played straight, as in Rossetti's *House of Life,* "a hundred sonnets on the theme of one lover's fight against time," the mind is given its victory in visionary claims like those of Tennyson in section XCV of *In Memoriam.* Time and change are abolished; the erotic moment sustains itself against all mortal erosions, suspends laws, defies death, creates its own space and time. But in *Porphyria's Lover,* in the redealing of the substitutions, the erotic and creative triumph is got through murder not vision. Death is the trump card. Inconstancy and belatedness are overcome by dealing death to the mistress—and to the precursor—controlling them forever. Both the lover who knows time and change are destroying his erotic bliss, and the poet who knows his poems are too late, achieve their desire by an act of violence—a victory as false as it is vain. The poem turns back against vision and against all experiential wisdoms, against the acceptance of sexual loss, against the solaces of the compensatory imagination. It is derisive and uncanny and has great sustaining energy, for if the dramatic monologues are indeed fictions about influence anxiety and the struggle of the poet to gain priority, then any poem which plays and works this theme, however indirectly, wins the poet some power over his creative anxieties and readies him for his open triumph over them.

This is not the standard description of the monologues. As *Johannes Agricola* was printed as a companion poem in the 1845 volume, it might be interesting to take a more orthodox look at this second of the pair. In such terms it is a typical dramatic monologue, and so in studying it we shall be dealing with what Robert Langbaum in *The Poetry of Experience* calls "empiricism in literature." "We might even say," he writes, "that the dramatic monologue takes as its material the literary equivalent of the scientific attitude—the equivalent being, when men and women are the subject of investigation, the historicizing and psychologizing of judgment." Hence Langbaum adds Johannes Agricola to Tennyson's St Simeon Stylites as another example of "religious buccaneering," and shows that "though Browning intends us to disapprove of Johannes' Antinomianism, he complicates the issue by showing the lofty passion that can proceed from the immoral doctrine." This brings the reader to the characteristic tension between sympathy and moral judgment which draws him into the dilemma of the monologue, loosening him from his customary moral certainties and offering him the new insights of an empiricist and relativist age. Thus we learn to read from within the material itself, no longer dependent on our own external standards of judgment. It is a logical development of romantic inwardness and is uniquely achieved as an effect of the form, "that extra quantity," Langbaum explains, "which makes the difference in artistic discourse between content and meaning."

Clearly the orthodox reading is very different from Bloom's, for whom "every poem . . . begins as an encounter *between poems*," for whom "acts, persons and places . . . must themselves be treated as though they were already poems, or part of poems. Contact, in a poem, means contact with another poem, even if that poem is called a deed, person, place or thing." Whether it is with the precursor, or the unconscious, or with both, this encounter engenders poetry, and to recall it restores the sense of Browning's uncanny energy, which the standard description reduces to lessons in nineteenth-century humanism.

In *Johannes Agricola* there is the same shift from literal to figurative as in *Porphyria's Lover*, and the same shuffling of effects, though this time they belong to religious and not erotic experience. Again the subject is not the imaginative triumph unmediated, but rather the triumph deliberately askewed. Johannes is God's child:

> For as I lie, smiled-on, full-fed
> > By inexhaustible power to bless,
> I gaze below on hell's fierce bed
> > And those its waves of flame oppress
> > Swarming in ghastly wretchedness:
> > Whose life on earth aspired to be
> One altar smoke, so pure—to win
> > If not love like God's love for me,
> At least to keep his anger in.

Do we really hesitate here between sympathy and judgment? Are we not rather drawn in by the recognition of desire to watch the speaker's impermissible bliss as he lies "smiled-on, full-fed," our envy pacified by the poet's acknowledgement? And through the displacement do we not glimpse the poet's desire for such a creative gratification that no rival can threaten him?

> Priest, doctor, hermit, monk grown white
> > With prayer, the broken hearted nun,
> The martyr, the wan acolyte,
> > The incense-swinging child—undone
> Before God fashioned star or sun!

And after all, isn't the poem really a brazen mimicry of Shelley's *Ode to the West Wind?*

The mysterious moment that Bloom places between 1840 and 1842 marks, not a change from solipsism to humanistic concerns, but a displacement of the dramas of creative life on to fictive substitutes. The movement is therefore not from a pastiche of Romanticism to an authentic Victorian voice, but from a poetry too dangerously open to desire and death to a deflection, screening, mimicking of the same themes—a movement towards the polymorphic, towards processes which play and replay the original themes through parallels and equivalences at a narrative level. It is not an ironisation of the early poems, a progress from delusion to insight. Sordello, like Alastor and Hyperion, dies, not as a punishment but as a gratification of desire. The pattern is a dangerously repetitious one—both a vicious circle and a dead-end—and if poetry were only the release of our primordial narcissism, it would perhaps always involve a surreptitious privileging of beautiful and enigmatic deaths. But great poems are not just narcissistic reveries, and Bloom's theory of revisionism is a powerful attempt at defining a creative process which is as necessary and constitutive to the writing of poetry as the Freudian dream-work is to the encounter with the unconscious. Hence the triumph of *Childe Roland* over both *Sordello* and the monologues.

Sooner or later, Browning realizes the creative cost of the early poems. He never devalued *Sordello* as a poem, and his fellow poets Swinburne and Rossetti read it deeply, but after it he realigned his material, displacing it onto all the substitutes, imitations, travesties of vatic intensities which flicker in and out of ordinary life—erotic and religious fantasies, deathbed reveries, self-projections, narcissisms. Browning shifts ground, not because he is too multifaceted and red-blooded to stay with Shelleyan idealism, but because poems like *Sordello*—unless achieved through the full processes of revisionism—can end only in submission to the deathwish. The shift produces a near-inexhaustible defensive play over the now latent theme, the same old one: the desire of the creative mind for priority. And if this is not Browning's greatest poetry, it is only because it is a play which brings him closer and closer to the moment in which the full revisionary process can be achieved.

HERBERT F. TUCKER, JR.

Cleon Orders His Urn

Death, death! It is this harping on death
I despise so much, this idle and often
cowardly as well as ignorant harping! Why
should we not change like everything else?
In fiction, in poetry, in so much of both,
French as well as English, and, I am told,
in American art and literature, the shadow
of death — call it what you will, despair,
negation, indifference — is upon us. But what
fools who talk thus! Why, amico mio, *you know*
as well as I that death is life, just as our
daily, our momentarily dying body is none the
less alive and ever recruiting new forces of
existence. Without death, which is our
crapelike churchyardy word for change, for
growth, there could be no prolongation of that
which we call life. Pshaw! it is foolish to
argue upon such a thing even. For myself, I
deny death as an end of everything. Never
say of me that I am dead!

—BROWNING to William Sharp

Browning knew as early as *Pauline* that artistic tradition is a fiction, perhaps an indispensable one, that is constituted and maintained by artists long before it is reconstituted by the custodians of artistic history. The fiction of artistic tradition, like any living fiction, is perennially subject to fresh interpretation. Browning revises Shelley as the Sun-treader, and Fra Lippo Lippi revalues the school of Giotto—each in order to place himself at the beginning of a new chapter in the history of art that he is engaged in writing. In "Cleon," Browning creates an artist who does just the opposite and inscribes himself into what he hopes will be a concluding paragraph: "Live long and happy, and in that thought die: / Glad for what was! Farewell" (336–37). Cleon is finally so "glad for what was," so happy with the task of imposing closure, and so uneasy with anything else, that he may be invited to perform that task here.

According to Cleon's overwhelmingly retrospective view of artistic tradition, he and his multifarious accomplishments in poetry, sculpture, painting, and music, "all my works wherein I prove my worth" (318), are worthy because of their climactic position. The meaning of artistic tradition coalesces in Cleon's sympathetic unification of the works of Homer, Terpander, Phidias, and other precursors, "running these into one soul" (144): "In such a synthesis the labour ends" (94). History stops with Cleon; and he evaluates his achievements by the ahistorical, neo-Aristotelian or proto-Arnoldian criteria of combination (60), composition (65), wholeness (77), and completeness (79). He sees the life of art steadily and sees it whole, because in his deliberate view that life has ceased to grow.

Whether or not Browning had anyone so specific as Arnold in mind for a model, the poem concerns itself less with Cleon's position than with the lyric play between that position and Cleon's motive for taking it up. A central and potent motive is the need to vindicate himself as an important artist. His fiction of artistic tradition satisfies this need by driving competing artists from his field of vision. Cleon's ideal of truncated progress lets him remain glad for what was by accommodating the works of earlier artists as partial achievements that anticipate his consummate integrity. He is a better artist because a later one, "For where had been the progress otherwise?" (91). At the same time, by calling a halt to progress in his entrenched present, he proleptically eliminates his successors from the running. The perfection of his works leaves nothing to be done by future artists: "How shall a certain part, pronounced complete, / Endure effacement by another part? / Was the thing done?—then, what's to do again?" (79–81). Like that other classicist, the Bishop at St. Praxed's (1845), Cleon orders his urn by denying the future; the dying Bishop's inability to recognize and bless his sons bespeaks a less somber version of the isolating impulse within this speaker.

Cleon's fiction of tradition is not the first such consoling fiction that he has made. His letter reveals that a need for artistic vindication has been with him for some time and has at least on one occasion directed his choice of a theme:

> And thus our soul, misknown, cries out to Zeus
> To vindicate his purpose in our life:
> Why stay we on the earth unless to grow?
> Long since, I imaged, wrote the fiction out,
> That he or other god descended here
> And, once for all, showed simultaneously
> What, in its nature, never can be shown,
> Piecemeal or in succession;—showed, I say,
> The worth both absolute and relative
> Of all his children from the birth of time,
> His instruments for all appointed work.
>
> (112–22)

Presumably this "fiction," like Cleon's fiction of tradition, justifies the comprehensiveness of his synthetic labors in "all appointed work." He invokes the descent of his deity in a critical rather than an inspirational capacity for the purpose of conducting a last judgment that includes "all his children from the birth of time." In Browning's poetry the birth of time is a potentially self-renewing process; but Cleon's fiction turns it into a forced march terminating now, "once for all," in the existence of Cleon as the last and most favored of children. Cleon's is a far cry from the cry of Paul at Athens in the verse from which Browning drew his epigraph for the poem: "For in him we live, and move, and have our being; as certain also of your own poets have said, For we are also his offspring" (Acts 17:28). In comparison with Paul's ecumenical life and movement, Cleon's desire for apocalyptic closure seeks fulfillment in what amounts to a curse of sterility banning further offspring.

Yet the fact that as a poet Cleon has to write his fiction out witnesses to the very fertility of time that he is eager to deny. He acknowledges what Sordello has had to acknowledge before him in a seminal passage, which Browning is rewriting here: that the attempt to render "the simultaneous and the sole / By the successive and the many" is doomed by the piecemeal temporality of language (*Sordello*, II.594–95). Good poems, and good fictions of artistic history for that matter, welcome their temporality and give it play; they owe their success to the use they make of time, to the dramatically unfolding variations and conflicts of which their stories consist. Cleon's reference to writing may remind a reader that this poem, one of Browning's few epistolary monologues, is not a transcription of speech but something originally written out. Despite the local color of its opening paragraphs and occasional later references to place, the poem is highly unlocalized. Its special status as a letter makes its voice more than usually disembodied for a Browning lyric and concentrates attention on the way it lives and moves in time. As Cleon marks the sequence of his letter, from a "first requirement" (42), through a "next" (158), to a "last point" (273), the letter proclaims itself "in its nature" a temporal document that defies his idea of simultaneity.

Organized as it is in time, the entire poem demands to be read against Cleon's overt intention to freeze time. The chilling drama of its local passages arises in his remorseless maneuvering to stabilize temporal energies and to overpower the hapless human yearnings that those energies represent. If Cleon cannot have simultaneity, he can at least have closure as the next-best thing. His cunning rhetoric reflects the closural bias of his view of artistic tradition; the privilege of finality is written into passage after passage in which imaginative possibilities are begotten, allowed brief play, and put to death. The strict will to interpretive closure that oversees Cleon's history of the arts also monitors the little histories constituted in the passages and sentences he writes. His monologue presents a glittering, consistently untrustworthy fabric of reductive self-interpretations; and to read it is to unravel the characteristic dramatic patterns that he knits in time.

Cleon's decidedly undramatic fiction of an aesthetic last judgment, for example, may assume a dramatic interest if one asks what happens in its course to the soulful cry with which it has begun: "Why stay we on the earth unless to grow?" Within a few lines Cleon drafts this disruptive question into the service of a philosophy denying further birth and growth: the passage reinterprets Zeus's "purpose in our life," initially an evolutionary intention, as an absolute goal appointed and achieved. As the passage goes on, Cleon practices further refinements in self-interpretation:

> I now go on to image,—might we hear
> The judgment which should give the due to each,
> Show where the labour lay and where the ease,
> And prove Zeus' self, the latent everywhere!
> This is a dream.

> (123–27)

This later fiction irons out what is implicit in its predecessor. All laborers receive their final due; the auditory "hear" of the first line gives place in the third to the visual display of "show"; and a spatially diffused, omnipresent Zeus no longer needs to take the trouble, or the time, to descend. The ultimate perversity of the passage is that Cleon undermines the independence of even so flattened a fiction: "This is a dream." Not content to dismiss his successors to artistic poverty, he dismisses to insignificance his more immediate progeny, his imaginative creations.

Cleon is quite right to hold himself aloof from fictional ways of meaning. He sees, and hates, what Fra Lippo Lippi sees in figuration and loves: its tendency to become a prefiguration intimating the future. Cleon repudiates his own fictions because he recognizes in the process of signification the greatest of threats to his desire for apocalyptic closure, and he measures his own power of finality by his ability to resist the opening power of the sign.

> Is it for Zeus to boast,
> "See, man, how happy I live, and despair—
> "That I may be still happier—for thy use!"
> If this were so, we could not thank our lord,
> As hearts beat on to doing: 't is not so—
> Malice it is not. Is it carelessness?
> Still, no. If care—where is the sign? I ask,
> And get no answer, and agree in sum,
> O king, with thy profound discouragement,
> Who seest the wider but to sigh the more.
> Most progress is most failure: thou sayest well.
> (262–72)

To "get no answer," as Browning tells Renan in the "Epilogue" to *Dramatis Personae* and lets Tertium Quid show in *The Ring and the Book,* is to get only too clear and premature an answer. Cleon's letter is formally an answer to Protus's questions and more intimately a succession of answers to his own questions about growth and progress:

> Was the thing done?—then what's to do again?
> (81)

> For where had been a progress, otherwise?
> (92)

> Why stay we on the earth unless to grow?
> (114)

> What, and the soul alone deteriorates?
> (138)

> Shall I go on a step, improve on this,
> Do more for visible creatures than is done?
> (195–96)

> Man might live at first
> The animal life: but is there nothing more?
> (214–15)

All of these lines offer variations upon the fundamentally Browningesque theme, is there nothing more? Protus may take Cleon's questions at face value, but Browning's reader must know better and must appreciate their function in Cleon's internal bids for power. The more repeatedly and comprehensively Cleon can assert that there is nothing more, the more confidently he will be asserting his own climactic position and saying, "I stand myself" (151). "Most progress is most failure" for Cleon because he defines himself through repeated denials of his own progressive impulses, through carefully staged scenes in which he releases those impulses only to watch them fail.

The greatest show of strength in this passage comes when Cleon denies the significance of the grateful impulse to "thank our lord," which is introduced at line 265. The economic notion of a responsive thanksgiving has the same liberating potential here as in "Fra Lippo Lippi," and Cleon's prospective phrase "as hearts beat on to doing" acknowledges this potential. As Paul's sermon to the Athenians puts it, God has so stationed humankind in time on the face of the earth "that they should seek the Lord, if haply they might feel after him, and find him, though he be not far from every one of us" (Acts 17:27). Paul's emphasis on feeling is shared by Browning, whose psychologized theology would teach that the cordial impulse of gratitude to Zeus is, in fact, the very "sign" of conviction that Cleon professes to be seeking when he asks, "Where is the sign?" But one underestimates both Cleon's ingenuity and Browning's if one fails to distinguish Cleon's professions from his motives. He seeks not the sign, but an invalidation of the sign, a semantic bankruptcy that will let him have the last word.

Cleon recognizes perfectly well that his impulse of gratitude is a sign, but he severely limits the extent of its meaning. He grants it only the negative power of showing that Zeus is not a malicious god; and then, at the precise moment of going further to posit the benevolence of Zeus, he effaces the sign and answers that there is no answer. For Cleon the gratifying theological consequence of this answer is that Zeus becomes neither malicious, nor careless, nor careful, but simply impotent, like Caliban's Setebos. Power devolves instead upon Cleon, who takes his stand on a willed designification of his heart's promptings so that he may enjoy the masterful self-importance of what is a literal disheartening: "profound discouragement." He opens out the vista of a freely responsive exchange between careful creator and thankful creature, only to shut it up in a conclusive response deepening the profundity of one who must preside at a summing up, one who must have all the answers. The penultimate line of the passage is a statement of Cleon's reductive purpose: he sees the wider in order to realize his stubborn intention to sigh the more.

Although for the most part Cleon's interpretive intention operates unobtrusively within his letter, in answering Protus's last point he makes that intention quite explicit. Protus has felicitated him on the superiority of an artist's survival to that of a king: "Thy life stays in the poems men shall sing" (170). Cleon's response to this threat of futurity is to upbraid Protus, twice, for confusing the figurative and literal meanings of "a word":

> The last point now:—thou dost except a case—
> Holding joy not impossible to one
> With artist-gifts—to such a man as I
> Who leave behind me living works indeed;
> For such a poem, such a painting lives.
> What? dost thou verily trip upon a word?
> (273–78)

> "But," sayest thou—(and I marvel, I repeat,
> To find thee trip on such a mere word) "what
> "Thou writest, paintest, stays; that does not die:
> "Sappho survives, because we sing her songs,
> "And Æschylus, because we read his plays!"
> (301–5)

The repetition of these defensive disclaimers is significant, as is the ambiguity of Cleon's "word," which may refer to either of two verbs in Protus's letter: "lives" (271) or "stays" (303). With this ambiguity Browning achieves a delicate balance between transcendental and descendental versions of the future: between the prophetic life everlasting preached by Paul as a new way of life in which the redeemed soul lives, and moves, and has its being; and the more literal secular permanence sought by pagan kings and artists, who would stay mutability by living through the works of an Ozymandias, a Protus, or a Cleon. It seems strange that Browning or his readers should expect Cleon to entertain seriously the possibility of accepting Christ. But the force of the poem does not really depend on such an expectation; for Cleon denies not just the future according to Paul, but even the future as offered on venerable pagan grounds. His rejection of Paul's word in the final verse paragraph is an afterthought confirming the reductive impulse behind his entire letter. He rejects the living word in both Christian and pagan senses because what he would purge from the word is its staying power, the elusive life of poetic figuration—the flaw in language upon which the ingenuous Protus has tripped towards the future as happily as the soliloquizing Spanish monk, and with a more naive grace.

Cleon's superbly terminal sophistication depends upon his ability to cover up that flaw, to assert literal over figurative meaning by demonstrating that any sign is "a mere word." He refuses to trip, as he refuses to stoop to Protus's inquiry about the early Christians: "Thou wrongest our philosophy, O king, / In stooping to inquire of such an one, / As if his answer could impose at all!" (346–48). The rival interpreter dismissed in these lines is the apostle Paul, the new master of an expansive, figural hermeneutics. Paul's willingness to begin reinterpreting the poetic word, as expressed in the fragmentary clause that heads this poem, recalls Cleon's chief rival in *Men and Women,* the physician Karshish, who ends his letter in the questioning mode of an interpretation poised on the verge of meaning: "The madman saith He said so: it is strange" ("An Epistle," 312). Cleon must at any cost protect himself against such barbarian beginnings. His philosophy of invincible finality, the temporal equivalent of the utter priority initially claimed by Paracelsus, Sordello, and every lyric speaker in Browning, demands answers that can "impose," answers placing a seal on figuration and suppressing its unruly fertility.

In burying the possibility of the sign, Cleon buries the future. The climactic paragraph of his letter anticipates with grim satisfaction the only future that his strict vision will admit: a literal burial.

> Thou diest while I survive?
> Say rather that my fate is deadlier still,
> In this, that every day my sense of joy
> Grows more acute, my soul (intensified
> In power and insight) more enlarged, more keen;
> While every day my hairs fall more and more,
> My hand shakes, and the heavy years increase—
> The horror quickening still from year to year,
> The consummation coming past escape
> When I shall know most, and yet least enjoy—
> When all my works wherein I prove my worth,
> Being present still to mock me in men's mouths,
> Alive still, in the praise of such as thou,
> I, I the feeling, thinking, acting man,
> The man who loved his life so over-much,
> Sleep in my urn.
> (308–23)

The swell of a fourteen-line sentence, in which Cleon has opened all the rhetorical stops, is suddenly stopped cold by the curt predicate of this last hemistich. Browning blunted the line both metrically and temporally by revising his 1855 reading, "Shall sleep in my urn." Browning's rhythmic revision enacts the foreshortening of tense whereby Cleon ruthlessly pulls his future, "alive still," into the fatal enclosure of the present.

In the lines that follow, Cleon practices his skill in combination and integration by bringing together the poem's major imaginative possibilities, and he savors his self-directed *Schadenfreude* by rejecting them all in a single, brutal "no!":

> It is so horrible,
> I dare at times imagine to my need
> Some future state revealed to us by Zeus,
> Unlimited in capability
> For joy, as this is in desire for joy,
> —To seek which, the joy-hunger forces us:
> That, stung by straitness of our life, made strait
> On purpose to make prized the life at large—
> Freed by the throbbing impulse we call death,
> We burst there as the worm into the fly,
> Who, while a worm still, wants his wings. But no!
> Zeus has not yet revealed it; and alas,
> He must have done so, were it possible!
>
> (323–35)

The creation of an imaginative fiction, the attribution of promising "purpose" to Zeus, the willingness to trust the heart's "throbbing impuse" as a sign transfiguring endings into beginnings—all return from earlier passages in Cleon's letter to be wrought into an eloquent prophecy. But Cleon admits the human need for a future, for an open question, only in order to impose his answer and enjoy its reductive force. Cleon prefers such harsh enjoyment to the "joy" he professes to desire, because he finally prefers the "horrible" to the "possible." He lives to be "stung by straitness of our life," by the astringent exercise of an imaginative asceticism. For Cleon the "need," the "desire," the "joy-hunger," and the "want" all answer to a deeper need: his need to identify power with closure, the "not yet revealed" with the unrevealable, the possible with the present. These necessitarian identities put an end not only to Cleon's imagined "future state," but to any meaningful future whatsoever.

"But no!" The glare of Cleon's defiant retrospect, illuminating the Hellenic tradition in art and his own career as its terminal artist, also lights up the contrasting accomplishments of Browning's early and middle years. Like Cleon, many of Browning's characters are grand refusers; but while Cleon forsakes the future for the present, they do quite the reverse. In *Pauline*, Browning says no to Shelley, and to the ideal of imaginative autonomy that his Shelley represents, for the sake of a future whose significance is at once religious and poetic. In *Paracelsus* and *Sordello*, he dramatizes the transformation of the ideal power of priority into the livelier currency of secondariness and anticipation; Paracelsus's protest against received definitions of the human and Sordello's against the given continuities of the natural order become pledges of definitions and orders yet to be. The apostate Strafford repeatedly denies his early allegiances as a way of establishing a later beginning. Browning's concentration on the making and marring of images in *Strafford* and other plays suggests that the poet's traffic with images of truth is but a special case of the deferential dynamics whereby all his men and woman recreate and maintain their worlds. "Artemis Prologizes" checks a grand refusal comparable to Cleon's by finding new possibilities outside the confines of the funeral pyre—the same pyre that to Cleon means only the dust and ashes of his own incineration, "The consummation coming past escape." And, for Fra Lippo Lippi, Artemis's lesson is second nature: he takes breath and tries to add life's flash, drawing inspiration from his sense of himself as a mutable man in a world poised in intimation. Lippo stands with Browning at the place of meaning, between the present and the future, the carnal and the holy, the secular and the divine.

In contrast to these and other figures, Cleon represents the imagination at once bound by its own grandeur and famished by a sense of insufficiency that can only drive it possessively back upon itself. In this Cleon resembles Browning's Duke; he is, indeed, the ducal reader turned artist and endowed with the greater self-knowledge that distinguishes the artist from the connoisseur. The Duke remains self-possessed by closing up his Duchess, and thus he illustrates the Browningesque paradox that untrammeled self-assertion results in a caricature of the living self. The wages of priority is deathlike entrapment behind a mask that is grotesque, in part, because unwittingly adopted. Cleon is less grotesque than he is horribly great, because he understands the logic of self-possession and pursues that logic to its irresistible conclusion in the vision of his own ashes asleep in their enclosing urn. This vision, the ultimate reduction of human potential, puts "the infinite within the finite" in a sense precisely antithetical to Browning's art. It represents all that his philosophy of the imperfect, and the violent and subtle ploys of his corresponding poetics, endeavor to contest.

Cleon's grand refusal of Browning's religion is also a refusal of

Browning's poetry. Its utter negativity provides one of the clearest insights in all Browning's writing into the correlative importance of creativity, possibility, and the sense of the future. The arc of the poet's career . . . suggests that he found the best resistance to Cleon's will to closure, the best defense of creativity, possibility, and the sense of the future, in the dramatic deference recommended by Fra Lippo's good angel. Against the formidably hard-headed insistence of Cleon's "But no!" Browning worked the angelic countercharm "Not so fast!" He wrote a lifetime of poetry out of the antiphony of these two imperative voices, poetry that survives today because he heeded both voices so persistently, and so inventively orchestrated their discords.

When classifying his dramatic lyrics for republication in 1863, Browning gave "Cleon" pride of place among "Men and Women" after all of the major monologues of the 1840s and 1850s, but he did not let it close the volume. The closing poem bears as its title what seems the inevitable last word for his art of disclosure: "One Word More." It makes little difference to Browning whether poetry is caught up in the radiant gyres of the self-involved sublime or encased within the formalist objectivity of Cleon's well-wrought urn; neither mode, in itself, will sustain the poetry of the future. If every meaning is already present, as the chilling hauteur of "Cleon" shows, there can be no word more and nothing to look forward to. There can be no more to say if all revelation is now.

STEVEN SHAVIRO

Browning upon Caliban upon Setebos . . .

*Those great poets . . . are and must be men of the moment, sensual,
absurd, fivefold, irresponsible, and sudden in mistrust and trust; with
souls in which they must usually conceal some fracture; often taking
revenge with their works for some inner contamination, often seeking
with their high flights to escape into forgetfulness from an all-too-
faithful memory; idealists from the vicinity of* swamps. . . .

—NIETZSCHE

"Caliban Upon Setebos" is one of
the most puzzlingly obscure of Browning's great dramatic monologues.
Despite the poem's obvious and immediate relevance to the great Victorian
debates over evolutionism and over religious revelation, its precise position within those debates is exceedingly difficult to ascertain. The poem
admits of an unusually wide range of readings; it has been interpreted
variously as a satire upon the Calvinist doctrine of predestination, as an
argument for the necessity of revelation, and as an optimistic account of
the development of the human religious sense. What is most striking,
however, is the way in which the poem itself dramatizes just such an
interpretative dilemma. The poet remains just as tantalizingly hidden from
the reader as Setebos does from Caliban, making a lapse into the intentional fallacy as unavoidable as it is indefensible; and the labyrinths of the

From *Browning Society Notes* 12 (1983). Copyright © 1983 by Steven Shaviro.

text baffle and resist the reader in much the same way that the labyrinths of nature baffle and resist Caliban's interpretative efforts.

Caliban himself may be most satisfactorily characterised as the obsessive interpreter *par excellence*. He reads nature as a text with a hidden author, and ceaselessly endeavors to fix within an elaborate interpretative scheme himself and everything he encounters. The major trope of "Caliban Upon Setebos" is the argument from design of natural theology. But reading the book of nature is no easy task for this mid-nineteenth-century savage theologian. Nature, on this island, is violent, unstable, and chaotic; Caliban is incessantly compelled to make new adjustments to his theories, and to put forth ever new analogies, in order to keep up with the unceasing flow of new ideas, facts, and experiences. He argues from a design which is constantly threatening to dissolve. Shakespeare's Caliban seemed to possess a fixed position upon the Great Chain of Being; whereas Browning's monster lives within an anarchy of competing forces.

It is in response to this impossibility of interpretation, this unlimited phenomenality, that theology becomes teleology, that essence is defined solely in terms of origin. Caliban strives to reduce chaos by discovering a hidden order and cause, and to account for his own being, and that of the universe around him, by determining what creative activity was the origin of himself and of his world. The trope of evolution first generates the figure of Caliban as primitive man, and is then adopted as Caliban's own method of reasoning. Browning returns us to the origins of theology, only to present us with a theology of origins. Such a transposition is inherent in any genetic interpretation: when essence is located in origin, origin itself becomes part of that unending process which is all that is left of essence, and is thereby subverted. There is an origin or ancestral point at the start of human existence, from which all of mankind has evolved; yet this origin is itself only a (missing) link, a mediator between ourselves and something even more ancient. Even (or especially) as a primitive man or representative of human origins, Caliban is already caught up in a process which exceeds and precedes him, as it is beyond his own control. The burden of the poem is thus that every origin must itself be accounted for in terms of something previous. Caliban must discover devious and round-about ways to account for himself and therefore to assert his own power, and his own theologizing therefore strangely re-enacts the very writing of the poem.

As a quester after his own origins, Caliban necessarily finds himself enclosed within the text of nature which he seeks to interpret. His ambiguous position is expressed most obviously in the dramatic situation of the poem. He seeks refuge in the cave in order to find the freedom which will allow him to assert himself, yet this enclosure is itself an ominous restriction on his freedom. The missing link "flat on his belly in the pit's much mire" (2) is himself a part of the natural order which he wishes to transcend. He "never speaks his mind save housed as now" (268), but the house is more a self-limitation than a protection against the elements. Caliban explicitly complains of having been created without adequate safeguards against external force:

> Who made them weak, meant weakness He might vex.
> Had He meant other, while His hand was in,
> Why not make horny eyes no thorn could prick,
> Or plate my scalp with bone against the snow,
> Or overscale my flesh 'neath joint and joint,
> Like an orc's armour? Ay,—so spoil His sport!
> He is the One now: only He doth all.
>
> (172–178)

Caliban's speculation here seems strangely to anticipate a key twentieth-century mythology of origins, that of Freud in *Beyond the Pleasure Principle*. The "armour" which Caliban lacks is that of the Freudian protective shield against stimuli, and may be related especially to Freud's grim warning: "*Protection against* stimuli is an almost more important function for the living organism than *reception of* stimuli." When the protective shield is breached the organism is overwhelmed by too great an influx of external force. The organism's attention is thereafter fixated upon the point at which this trauma occurred: a primal repression motivated by a preceding experience of anxiety. Compulsive repetition will then be required to gain mastery over the excess of excitation.

In "Caliban Upon Setebos," enclosure is a concrete representation of the fixation which results from being overmastered by a superior power. There is already a precedent for this in *The Tempest*, in which Sycorax imprisons Ariel within a pine. In Browning's poem, Caliban's situation is only a less extreme version of that of the newt which Setebos "may have envied once/ And turned to stone, shut up inside a stone" (214–215). Just as being painfully enclosed is a consequence of defeat by a superior force, so enclosing something else, by overwhelming it with one's own force, is a prerogative of power. Caliban himself encloses the things of the isle which are inferior to him as he is to Setebos: " 'Wove wattles half the winter, fenced them firm/ With stone and stake to stop she-tortoises/ Crawling to lay their eggs here" (205–207). Superior skill and strength, manifested in a creative act of making and enclosing, interfere with the tortoises' pursuit of the pleasure principle in the form of the organic act of generation. Setebos's destruction of this tortoise-trap reminds Caliban of the extent to which he is enclosed within a nature greater than himself, rather than being one of those who enclose others.

The same pattern of enclosure and fixation also determines the act of speech which constitutes the main body of the poem. Caliban's speaking is or should be an organic process, "letting the rank tongue blossom into speech" (23) like a marsh flower. But such organicism is largely an illusion. Language is not natural, but was taught Caliban (according to *The Tempest*) by Prospero and Miranda. More directly, Caliban's actual speech is enclosed within the poem by the bracketed opening and closing verse-paragraphs, in which he thinks but does not give his thoughts utterance. The only two real events in the poem, Caliban's withdrawal into the cave and the coming of the storm, occur during these bracketed passages; while it is only the absence of strong events and stimuli that makes it possible for Caliban to give free rein to his verbal speculations. The storm arrives as "a curtain o'er the world at once" (284), a curtain whose descent also signals the end of Caliban's dramatic performance. Speech, ideally organic, can in fact only be permitted to blossom forth when external dangers have temporarily withdrawn. The force of external nature, personified in Setebos, disrupts Caliban's natural exertion through speech, just as Caliban's own striving for mastery disrupts for a time the natural generative acts of the tortoises.

Thus Caliban's act of speaking, enclosed both spatially and temporally, is necessarily embedded in mazes of futility and self-contradiction. Through speech he achieves in phantasy a freedom, impossible in reality, from the constrictions of nature, or of Setebos's will. But in the long run Setebos overhears him, and in consequence renews and intensifies his punishments. Caliban is like the "great fish" enclosed within the net of "yon sea which sunbeams cross/ And recross till they weave a spider-web": he "breaks at times" those "meshes of fire" but inevitably falls back into the sea (12–14). A quotation from the Fiftieth Psalm serves as a motto for the entire poem, but a later verse from that same Psalm more thoroughly indicates Caliban's predicament: "to him that ordereth his conversation aright will I show the salvation of God" (Ps. 50:23). For Caliban this injunction is an impossible double bind, since his speech is all too ordered (oriented towards Setebos) already, and yet can never be ordered "aright." "You taught me language, and my profit on't/ Is, I know how to curse" (*The Tempest*, I, ii, 363–364). Caliban's relative powerlessness organizes his speech in terms of a traumatic fixation: he can speak of nothing but "Setebos, Setebos, and Setebos!" (24). The role of such speech is to bind and master a too-powerful impulse, to overcome the external force (Setebos) which is oppressing the speaker. The more Caliban orders his speech toward Setebos, the less that speech will please Him. The impossibility of this situation is reflected in Caliban's remarkable confusion about the effects of his discourse: "to talk about Him, vexes—ha!/ Could He but know!" (17–18). He cannot avoid discussing Setebos, and therefore can win a relative freedom only by vexing Him; but he can only escape Setebos's wrath, and thus maintain a modicum of freedom, if Setebos does not know that He is being vexed. Caliban's speech is an entirely solipsistic activity (he "talks to his own self, howe'er he please"—15) which nevertheless not only refers to Setebos incessantly ("touching that other"—16), but even postulates Setebos as an inevitable audience. Caliban compulsively attempts both to please and to vex Setebos, when true freedom could consist only in doing neither.

Such a confusion is inevitable, since in his fixation Caliban transforms everything which he experiences or imagines, external or internal, into a simile for Setebos: "So He." In the repetitive process of mastering the trauma of his encounter with the manifestations of Setebos's power, he transforms himself into a metaphorical reduction, and repetition, of his creator. The processes of imagining Setebos (constituting Him in Caliban's own image through natural theology) and of mastering Setebos (mastering the powerful stimuli from outside) are equivalent to one another and to the process of becoming more and more enslaved to Setebos. From this perspective, it becomes irrelevant whether Caliban has invented Setebos, or Setebos Caliban. In either case, the closest analogy to Caliban's natural theology is the process which William Blake referred to as natural religion, the self-entrapping argument from design of the speaker of "The Tyger."

Setebos is so much more powerful than Caliban that aggression flows only in one direction. In Freudian terms, undischarged excitation, which the mind experiences as unpleasure, is nevertheless necessary to life: hence Caliban could be said to exist precisely to the extent that Setebos is torturing him. To be created and to be tortured are both aspects of being enclosed or confined, are in fact one and the same. Setebos is fixated upon as an origin because Caliban owes everything to Him, both positive and negative, but cannot affect Him in return. Caliban is relatively powerless, and his attempts at revenge and aggression are necessarily inhibited. If he can only vex Setebos in secret, this is structurally equivalent to a repression (in the Freudian sense) of the act of vexing Him. Similarly, when Caliban "mainly dances on dark nights/ . . . gets under holes to laugh,/ And never speaks his mind save housed as now" (267–269), he is buying the luxury of defiance only by insuring that such defiance will have no effect. Barring external contingencies, the fixity of his situation cannot be overcome: "here are we,/ And there is He, and nowhere help at all" (249).

Yet Caliban is far less miserable than one might expect him to be, given the hardships which he has to endure. He describes Setebos's actions as being usually sadistic and brutal; but he enjoys such descriptions, since within them he uses similes to present himself by analogy in an active role, rather than in the position of a passive victim. In psychoanalytic terms, these similes exemplify the defense mechanism which Anna Freud has called identification with the aggressor. Caliban cannot directly attack Setebos; but he can maintain an active role, and master and discharge excess excitation, by turning his aggression outward and downward against his own inferiors or victims. Caliban evades, for the moment, his fearful indebtedness to Setebos, by bringing forth (in verbal phantasy and in his acts) a new parody-creation in which he himself becomes the master of a helpless and dependent slave:

> Also [he has] a sea-beast, lumpish, which he snared,
> Blinded the eyes of, and brought somewhat tame,
> And split its toe-webs, and now pens the drudge
> In a hole o' the rock and calls him Caliban;
> A bitter heart that bides its time and bites.
>
> (163–167)

The sea-beast is enclosed "in a hole o' the rock" just as Caliban is enclosed in his cave; its physical blindness is equivalent to Caliban's blindness concerning Setebos's motivations and demands upon him. Caliban's activity has its analogue in Freud's famous observation about the repetition of unpleasant experiences in children's games: "As the child passes over from the passivity of the experience to the activity of the game, he hands on the disagreeable experience to one of his playmates and in this way revenges himself on a substitute." But as Caliban resembles Setebos and the sea-beast resembles Caliban, the context of such repetition is not innocuous play but a deadly series in which aggression is passed down from one "Caliban" to the next. Caliban survives only by making himself into a parody of Setebos, but similarly Setebos himself is merely a parodic creator, rather than a true origin: making "a bauble-world to ape yon real,/ These good things to match those as hips do grapes" (147–148).

Existence therefore is never in itself originary or "real," nor can it ever coincide with what it regards as its privileged origins. All action is obsessive repetition, the involuntary copying of a repressed (inaccessible or pragmatically non-existent) original. Even the most joyous act of creation is then a manifestation of the death instinct, motivated by hidden spite, and can scarcely be anything but a catastrophic destruction as well. Caliban's very existence is defined by his primal fixation upon the figure of Setebos, compelling him always bitterly to repeat Setebos in the act of defiantly parodying Him; and this act of creation/destruction must itself be repeated incessantly, since it cannot satisfy for more than a moment. Caliban can find no rest, but must rather continue to bring forth simile after simile in which he places himself in Setebos's role. "No use at all i' the work, for work's sole sake;/ 'Shall some day knock it down again: so He" (198–199).

The conjunction here of repetition and aggression is of course no accident. The poem traverses the same route by which Freud first postulated the death instinct in *Beyond the Pleasure Principle*. According to Freud, repetition as the mastering of stimuli is an instinctual process striving "to restore an earlier state of things" before the tension of an undischarged excitation disturbed the organism. But since "inanimate things existed before living ones," and since undischarged excitation is equivalent to life itself, the ultimate unexcited or pre-excited state is death, when internal tension is absolutely reduced to zero. Caliban's aggressive repetitions may therefore be regarded as functions of a drive to return to the death- or Nirvana-state which prevailed before he was created, before he was constituted as such by the disturbing influx reaching him from Setebos.

Freud's description of the Nirvana-state of constant or zero excitation, which the organism seeks through repetition, strangely resembles Caliban's conception of the ultimate divinity lying even beyond Setebos, or what he calls the Quiet:

> . . . the something over Setebos
> That made Him, or He, may be, found and fought,
> Worsted, drove off, and did to nothing, perchance.
> There may be something quiet o'er His head,
> Out of His reach, that feels not joy nor grief,
> Since both derive from weakness in some way.
> I joy because the quails come; would not joy
> Could I bring quails here when I have a mind:
> This Quiet, all it hath a mind to, doth.
>
> (129–137)

The Quiet subsists at an unchanging level of excitation, since it feels neither pleasure nor pain, which are the release and build-up of excitation respectively. Its lack of "weakness" is a lack of any gap between desire and fulfillment, which really means the absence of any desire. Caliban skeptically suggests that "it may look up, work up" (140): but even if it does so, such activity is of no concern to him, because it is so distant, and because such working, unlike Setebos's, is not driven by discomfort or necessity.

The Quiet is as far above Setebos as it is above Caliban, since in its neutrality it embodies the Nirvana-state towards which they both strive. Caliban and Setebos are essentially similar, since the former is a parody and repetition of the latter; but this implies a prior activity which Setebos is repeating and which is responsible for His discomfort: Setebos must also have a predecessor. Caliban's theology implies an infinite regress of creators, just as Darwinian theory would imply an infinite series of ancestors for Caliban. Every seeming origin is actually the successor of a yet earlier origin. The only way to cut off such an infinite series is to postulate the zero- or Nirvana-state not only as goal, but also as ultimate starting point. Since any possible experience of life is already mediate, death or nothingness must be both the origin and the aim of all life.

Thus Caliban's theologizing reaches a thoroughly nihilistic conclusion even before he is routed by the coming of the storm. Such nihilism is the pragmatic consequence of Caliban's quest after lost origins, of what may be called, in Nietzsche's happy phrase, his "idealis[m] from the vicinity of *swamps.*" But the Calibanish perspective from below also suggests the opposed and concurrent possibility of a perspective from above. There is a fruitful equivocation in the poem's description of Setebos. He is the model in accordance with which Caliban molds his own behavior, through the defense mechanism of identification with the aggressor. But He is also related to Caliban as the creator is related to the work which he has created. What is obsessive fixation from Caliban's point of view is active enclosure from Setebos's, the enclosure which is also the molding of a work of art. In suggesting such a perspective from above, "Caliban Upon Setebos" makes of theology a self-reflexive metaphor for its own processes, or for the process of artistic creation in general. The active work of creation complements the nihilistic and reactive work of obsessive interpretation.

"Natural theology" means that in the absence of revealed writings, Caliban reads nature itself as a text. But insofar as he imitates Setebos, Caliban is something of a sculptor or an architect (186–199); and he evades Setebos's dominion at one point specifically by writing a poem (275ff). All creative activity is necessarily catastrophic, but viewed from the opposite perspective this means that any outpouring of the aggressive instinct or will-to-power results in a well-wrought urn in which some inferior being, Caliban or the newt, is enclosed. The created being faces destruction exactly to the extent that it has been brought into being, not in accordance with any comforting evolutionist teleology, but "for work's sole sake" (198). Thus Caliban's fixation upon Setebos, and Setebos's binding of Caliban within a work of art, are the same event seen from opposing, high and low, perspectives.

Another formulation borrowed from psychoanalysis may make it easier to trace these opposed but intertwined perspectives. Setebos can be defined, within Caliban's psychic economy, as a repressive paternal imago; but He overpowers Caliban so completely that no true Oedipal conflict is possible. The psychic analogue to Caliban's situation is that of the male child's abandonment of his Oedipal desires due to fear of castration at the hands of the all-powerful father. Freud says in *The Ego and the Id* that this smashing of the Oedipus Complex is accomplished through identification with the previously hated figure of the interdicting father, who is transformed into the repressing superego. Anna Freud adds in *The Ego and the Mechanisms of Defence* that this identification is initially an identification with the aggressor. At first, the subject identifies with the father and projects the self-as-victim outward; only later is the formation of the superego completed, when the self becomes victim as well as aggressor.

We shall see that this equation of Setebos with the superego works only up to a certain point. But it is a useful analogy because the superego lies at the center of Freud's theory of guilt. The superego creates undeserved guilty feelings because it perpetuates the harsh demands of the external authority figure from whom it derives, but without distinguishing between real acts and mere thoughts and intentions. It will punish the ego whenever it detects the existence of a forbidden instinct, even if the ego has explicitly renounced that instinct. Caliban gains nothing when he inhibits his instinctual aggressiveness by talking, laughing, and dancing only in secret. Such a disavowal or repression is meaningless to the superego, which possesses complete insight into the ego. No matter what precautions Caliban takes, Setebos will always succeed in overhearing him or in spying upon him. Caliban is as unable to evade Setebos as to strike back at him.

The one-way relationship between Setebos and Caliban relates also to another aspect of Freud's theory of guilt. The superego acquires the energy with which it punishes the ego and creates feelings of guilt precisely by taking over instinctual aggression which has been repressed, and turning that aggression against the ego. The more virtuous and self-sacrificing the ego is in its attempts to placate the superego, the more the aggressive instinct is repressed and handed over to the superego, the more sadistically the superego rages, and the more guilty the ego feels. In this sense Caliban is his own torturer. When he hides or represses his aggression, he not only fails to avert punishment, but on the contrary makes his punishment all the more dreadful, since he ascribes to Setebos all the aggression which he has himself repressed. Caliban's masochistic turning against himself at the end of the poem thus only increases his burden of impotent hatred and resentment. In the ironically creative act of in turn tormenting his own inferiors, Caliban at once discharges this burden and reaffirms it, in an endless cycle of accumulation and discharge, a spiral of ever-increasing guilt.

Thus the structure of guilt is clearly articulated by the poem, even when the affect of guilt is not directly present within Caliban's discourse. Nietzsche's discussion of guilt in the Second Essay of On the Genealogy of Morals becomes at this point more relevant than Freud's theorizings, as Nietzsche traces guilt back to the more primitive situation of contractual indebtedness. The debt of Caliban the primitive man to his supposed creator is indeed immense. He owes his very existence to Setebos's whims; Setebos is not only his origin or maker, but also the source of every benefit (as well as every hurt) which he continues to experience. Thus the poem quite strikingly anticipates Nietzsche's fundamental insight into the psychology and anthropology of religion:

> The conviction reigns that it is only through the sacrifices and accomplishments of the ancestors that the tribe *exists*—and that one has to *pay them back* with sacrifices and accomplishments: one thus recognizes a *debt* that constantly grows greater, since these forebears never cease, in their continued existence as powerful spirits, to accord the tribe new advantages and new strength . . . the ancestors . . . are bound eventually to grow to monstrous dimensions through the imagination of growing fear and to recede into the darkness of the divinely uncanny and unimaginable: in the end the ancestor must necessarily be transfigured into a *god*. Perhaps this is even the origin of the gods, an origin therefore out of *fear*!

Guilt, fear, and indebtedness are at the root of Caliban's nihilistic perspective from below, and as such they also produce the illusion of the independence of the gods, the opposed perspective from above. Nietzsche remarks that "what really arouses indignation against suffering is not suffering as such but the senselessness of suffering." Setebos's supreme arbitrariness is the problem which vexes Caliban the most: "You must not know His ways, and play Him off,/ Sure of the issue" (224–225). Caliban's power of speculation is stretched to the utmost, as he can account for Setebos's whims only by asserting his own unaccountability in similar circumstances:

> 'Thinketh, such shows nor right nor wrong in Him,
> Nor kind, nor cruel: He is strong and Lord.
> 'Am strong myself compared to yonder crabs

> That march now from the mountain to the sea;
> 'Let twenty pass, and stone the twenty-first,
> Loving not, hating not, just choosing so.
> 'Say, the first straggler that boasts purple spots
> Shall join the file, one pincer twisted off;
> 'Say, this bruised fellow shall receive a worm,
> And two worms he whose nippers end in red;
> As it likes me each time, I do: so He.
>
> (98–108)

As Nietzsche further observes, punishment comes first, and the meaning or purpose of that punishment is only "*projected* and interpreted *into* the procedure" subsequently. Here the analogy between Setebos (or Caliban in relation to the crabs) and the superego breaks down: the superego, no matter how cruel, still enforces standards of recognizable right and wrong. Caliban, on the other hand, imitating Setebos, seems gratuitously sadistic because his actions, although carried through with ruthless exactitude, cannot be explained or predicted in advance. His commands are willful at the same time that they are arbitrary: he parcels out rewards and punishments on the basis of arbitrary and impermanent standards, factors which can be stated concretely, but which conform to no order and which the crabs can neither control nor even always discern. Right and wrong are here merely utilitarian standards which have meaning only from the standpoint of the victim: they do not inhere in actions, but are matters of interpretation. Caliban "supposeth [Setebos] is good i' the main,/ Placable if His mind and ways are guessed" (109–110), which is to say placable and good precisely to the extent that His mind and ways can be guessed. But in reality He is or appears to be implacable, since His mind and ways cannot possibly be guessed. Caliban, in a state of interpretative blindness, or reactive weakness, likes only what profits him, whereas Setebos's superior power releases Him from any such calculations and places Him in a non-utilitarian realm, one beyond good and evil (179–184).

Such mastery is a purely aesthetic state in which interpretability or the lack of it is no longer a problem, since the superior power can impose interpretations at will. Caliban treats the crabs as if they were merely counters in an abstract pattern of symmetries and discords, red patches and purple spots. Kindness and cruelty are alike impossible in the absence of any reciprocity in the relationship. A figure who is "strong and Lord" simply manipulates the beings who are under his authority. The crabs are unable to escape by interpreting; but Caliban's rewards and punishments alike represent the unrestrained activity of his own interpretative will-to-power. The artist's total control over his materials is equivalent to what

Freud describes in a different context as "a pure culture of the death instinct." Caliban's actions are deliberate and not random, even though the crabs cannot find any order in them. They express a triumph of that force which is the will to interpret, but at the expense of any particular interpretation. Caliban's treatment of the crabs is a manifestation of the pure aesthetic state of purposiveness without purpose.

Such an empty purposiveness is what unites the perspectives of victim and aggressor, of below and above, in their common derivation from the guilt of indebtedness. To quote Nietzsche yet again, "man would rather will *nothingness* than *not* will." Even randomness must be assigned a purpose. Caliban's first act of interpretation—motivated from his position as victim—is to postulate Setebos as the origin and cause of whatever discomforts and anxieties he suffers. The interpretative drive for mastery is thus itself only a product of the negative, deprived, reactive state of misery and lack. Caliban's first act of natural theologizing does not free him from the greater purposelessness of being trapped as a passive victim of what he regards as Setebos's inscrutable designs. A more active response becomes necessary. Mastery is achieved, after a fashion. But such mastery is itself still tied, in obsessive repetition, to the condition of deprivation and lack which motivates it. The drive for possession and domination is itself merely a nihilistic and reactive force, that which Nietzsche depre-cates under the name of slave morality. Caliban's immense purposiveness can only culminate in a monstrous hypostatization of death, since it has no purpose, no concrete object and aim, in the real world. Caliban remains the victim of his swampy idealism. When the power of random-ness, which is life itself, is fearfully apprehended from afar, separated from the subject, resisted, and secondarily appropriated, then creation can only be spun out over a void. The instinct of misery and negation cannot ultimately be distinguished from its seeming opposite, the passive nihilism of will-less and disinterested contemplation. Caliban's purposive aggres-siveness is a force which cannot affirm, which destroys whatever it creates or encounters, and which must end by even annihilating Caliban himself. By the fatality of the Nirvana principle, seemingly erratic and capricious behavior leads to a single conclusion of absolute fixity. The modernity of "Caliban Upon Setebos," its relevance to the intellectual and social movements not only of its time but of our own, lies in the rigor with which it poses the questions of the advent of nihilism, of the collapse of idealistic values, of the death of God. Whether Robert Browning ever moves beyond this negative point, whether his poetry is *also* the uncanny harbinger of a new affirmation, is a question which exceeds the limits of the present essay.

Chronology

1812	Born May 7 in Camberwell, near London, to Robert Browning and Sarah Anna Wiedemann Browning.
1820–26	Educated near home in boarding school.
1826	Conversion to Shelley and his poetry.
1828	Studied at new University of London, but gave it up after a brief period.
1833	Anonymous publication of his Shelleyan poem, *Pauline.*
1834	Travels to Russia.
1835	*Paracelsus* published.
1837	Production of his play, *Strafford.*
1838	First trip to Italy.
1840	*Sordello* published, to bad critical reception.
1841	*Pippa Passes* published.
1842	*Dramatic Lyrics* published.
1844	Second trip to Italy.
1845	*Dramatic Romances and Lyrics* published.
1845–46	Romance of Robert Browning and the poet Elizabeth Barrett. On January 10, 1845, Browning wrote his first letter to her, she being then a famous poet (more than he, at that point) but a psychic invalid, living with her notoriously possessive father, who refused to allow any of his children to marry. On May 20, 1845, Browning first called upon Miss Barrett at Wimpole Street. On September 12, 1846, after many mutual postponements, they eloped to the Continent.
1847	After moving about in Italy, the Brownings settled permanently at Casa Guidi, in Florence.
1849	First collected edition of Browning's work published. Birth of son, and death of Browning's mother.
1855	Browning's first masterpiece, *Men and Women,* published.
1861	Death of Elizabeth Barrett Browning on June 29.
1862	Returns to live in London.
1864	Publishes *Dramatis Personae,* his second masterwork, to considerable acclaim.
1866	Death of Browning's father.

1868–69   Publication of *The Ring and the Book,* his third great achievement, to remarkable public reception.

1879   *Dramatic Idyls* published.

1881   Founding of the Browning Society in London.

1888–89   Publication of sixteen volumes of *Poetical Works.*

1889   On December 12, *Asolando* published in London; that evening the poet dies at his son's house in Venice. On December 31, burial takes place in Westminster Abbey.

Contributors

HAROLD BLOOM, Sterling Professor of the Humanities at Yale University, is the author of *The Anxiety of Influence, Poetry and Repression* and many other volumes of literary criticism. His forthcoming study, *Freud: Transference and Authority*, attempts a full-scale reading of all of Freud's major writings. He is the general editor of *The Chelsea House Library of Literary Criticism*.

ROBERT LANGBAUM is James Branch Cabell Professor of English at the University of Virginia. His critical works include *The Poetry of Experience, The Modern Spirit* and *The Mysteries of Identity*.

ISOBEL ARMSTRONG is Professor of English at the University of Sussex. She has published extensively on Browning and on Victorian literature in general.

GEORGE M. RIDENOUR is Professor of English at the Graduate School of the City University of New York. He is the author of *The Style of "Don Juan."*

JOHN HOLLANDER, Professor and Director of Graduate Studies in English at Yale, is a poet and critic of high reputation. His most recent books are *Rhyme's Reason, Spectral Emanations: New and Selected Poems* and *The Figure of Echo*.

ELEANOR COOK is Professor of English at the University of Toronto. Besides her *Browning's Lyrics*, she is the author of a forthcoming study of Wallace Stevens.

ANN WORDSWORTH teaches English at St. Hughs College, Oxford University, where she is one of the editors of the *Oxford Literary Review*. Her work includes articles on Derrida and on literary theory.

HERBERT F. TUCKER, JR. teaches English at Northwestern University. He is the author of *Browning's Beginnings: The Art of Disclosure*.

STEVEN SHAVIRO teaches English at the University of Washington. His work includes articles on modern poetry and on critical theory.

Bibliography

Altick, Richard Daniel. *Browning's Roman Murder Story: A Reading of 'The Ring and the Book.'* Chicago: The University of Chicago Press, 1968.

————, ed. *Robert Browning: The Ring and the Book.* New Haven: Yale University Press, 1981.

Armstrong, Isobel, ed. *Writers and their Background: Robert Browning.* Athens: Ohio University Press, 1975.

Blackburn, Thomas. *Robert Browning, A Study of his Poetry.* London: Eyre and Spottiswoode, 1967.

Bloom, Harold, and Adrienne Munich, eds. *Robert Browning: A Collection of Critical Essays.* Englewood Cliffs, N. J.: Prentice-Hall, 1979.

Chesterton, G. K. *Robert Browning.* London: Macmillan, 1903.

Cook, Eleanor. *Browning's Lyrics: An Exploration.* Toronto: University of Toronto Press, 1974.

Crowell, Norton B. *The Convex Glass: The Mind of Robert Browning.* Albuquerque: University of New Mexico Press, 1968.

————. *Browning's Theory of Knowledge.* Albuquerque: University of New Mexico Press, 1963.

————. *A Reader's Guide to Browning.* Albuquerque: University of New Mexico Press, 1972.

De Vane, William Clyde, and Knickerbocker, Kenneth Leslie, eds. *New Letters.* New Haven: Yale University Press, 1950.

Drew, Philip. *The Poetry of Browning: A Critical Introduction.* London: Methuen, 1970.

Duckworth, Francis F. G. *Browning: Background and Conflict.* Hamden, Conn.: Archon Books, 1966.

Erickson, Lee. *Robert Browning: His Poetry and Audiences.* Ithaca: Cornell University Press, 1984.

Flowers, Betty S. *Browning and the Modern Tradition.* London: Macmillan, 1976.

Gridley, Roy E. *Browning.* London: Routledge and Kegan Paul, 1972.

Griffin, William Hall. *The Life of Robert Browning.* Hamden, Conn.: Archon Books, 1966.

Harrold, William. *The Variance and the Unity: A Study of the Complementary Poems of Robert Browning.* Athens: Ohio University Press, 1973.

Honan, Park. *Browning's Characters: A Study in Poetic Technique.* Hamden, Conn.: Archon Books, 1969.

Irvine, William. *The Book, the Ring and the Poet.* New York: McGraw Hill, 1974.

Johnson, Edward D. H. *The Alien Vision of Victorian Poetry: Sources of the Poetic*

Imagination in Tennyson, Browning and Arnold. Hamden, Conn.: Archon Books, 1963.

King, Roma A. *The Focusing Artifice: The Poetry of Robert Browning.* Athens: Ohio University Press, 1968.

———. *The Bow and the Lyre: The Art of Robert Browning.* Ann Arbor: University of Michigan Press, 1957.

King, Roma A., et al., eds. *The Complete Works of Robert Browning.* Athens: Ohio University Press, 1969.

Kintner, Elvan, ed. *The Letters of Robert Browning and Elizabeth Barrett Browning, 1845–1846.* Cambridge: Belknap Press, 1969.

Litzinger, Boyd. *The Browning Critics.* Lexington: University of Kentucky Press, 1965.

Litzinger, Boyd, and Smalley, Donald, eds. *Browning: The Critical Heritage.* London: Routledge and Kegan Paul, 1970.

Maynard, John. *Browning's Youth.* Cambridge: Harvard University Press, 1977.

Miller, Betty Bergson. *Robert Browning: A Portrait.* New York: Scribners, 1953.

Pettigrew, John, ed. *The Poems.* New Haven: Yale University Press, 1981.

Ricks, Christopher, ed. *The Brownings, Letters and Poetry.* Garden City, N. Y.: Doubleday, 1970.

Ridenour, George M., ed. *Robert Browning: Selected Poetry.* New York: New American Library, 1966.

Ryals, Clyde de L. *Browning's Later Poetry, 1871–1889.* Ithaca: Cornell University Press, 1975.

———. *Becoming Browning: The Poems and Plays of Robert Browning, 1833–1846.* Columbus: Ohio State University Press, 1983.

Shaw, William David. *The Dialectical Temper: The Rhetorical Art of Robert Browning.* Ithaca: Cornell University Press, 1968.

Smith, Margaret, and Jack Ian, eds. *The Poetical Works of Robert Browning.* New York: Oxford University Press, 1983.

Sullivan, Mary Rose. *Browning's Voices in 'The Ring and the Book': A Study of Method and Meaning.* Toronto: University of Toronto Press, 1969.

Thomas, Donald. *Robert Browning: A Life Within Life.* London: Weidenfield and Nicholson, 1982.

Tucker, Herbert F. *Browning's Beginnings: The Art of Disclosure.* Minneapolis: University of Minnesota Press, 1980.

Acknowledgments

"Introduction" by Harold Bloom from *Poetry and Repression: Revisionism from Blake to Stevens* by Harold Bloom, copyright © 1976 by Yale University. Reprinted by permission.

"The Dramatic Monologue: Sympathy versus Judgment" by Robert Langbaum from *The Poetry of Experience: The Dramatic Monologue in Modern Literary Tradition* by Robert Langbaum, copyright © 1957 by W. W. Norton. Reprinted by permission of Robert Langbaum.

"Mr. Sludge, 'The Medium' " by Isobel Armstrong from *Victorian Poetry*, vol. 2. (1964), copyright © 1964 by West Virginia University. Reprinted by permission of *Victorian Poetry*.

"Four Modes in the Poetry of Robert Browning" by George M. Ridenour from *Selected Poetry of Robert Browning*, edited by George M. Ridenour, copyright © 1966 by George M. Ridenour. Reprinted by permission.

"Browning: The Music of Music" by John Hollander from *Striver's Row* 1 (1974), copyright © 1974 by John Hollander. Reprinted by permission of John Hollander.

" 'Love Among the Ruins' " by Eleanor Cook from *Browning's Lyrics: An Exploration* by Eleanor Cook, copyright © 1974 by University of Toronto Press. Reprinted by permission.

" 'Childe Roland' " by Harold Bloom from *A Map of Misreading* by Harold Bloom, copyright © 1975 by Oxford University Press. Reprinted by permission.

"Browning's Anxious Gaze" by Ann Wordsworth from *Robert Browning: A Collection of Critical Essays*, edited by Harold Bloom and Adrienne Munich, copyright © 1979 by Ann Wordsworth. Reprinted by permission.

"Cleon Orders His Urn" by Herbert F. Tucker, Jr. from *Browning's Beginnings: The Art of Disclosure* by Herbert F. Tucker, Jr., copyright © 1980 by University of Minnesota Press. Reprinted by permission of University of Minnesota Press.

"Browning upon Caliban upon Setebos . . ." by Steven Shaviro from *Browning Society Notes* 12 (1983), copyright © 1983 by Steven Shaviro. Reprinted by permission.

Index